For Mornee and Rocio

Indonesia – Paradise on the Equator

TIMES EDITIONS
1 New Industrial Road
Singapore 536196

© 1987 Times Editions Pte Ltd
First published 1987
Reprinted 1989, 1992, 1996

Typeset by Superskill, Singapore
Colour separation by Daiichi, Singapore
and Far East Offset, Malaysia
Printed in Singapore
All rights reserved for all countries.

ISBN 981-204-085-4

The passage from *The Malay Archipelago* by Alfred Russel
Wallace is reprinted with permission of Dover Publications,
Inc. The passages from *A History of South-East Asia* by
D.G.E. Hall are reproduced with permission of St. Martin's
Press, Inc. The passage from *Sri Sumarah and Other Stories*
is by permission of Heinemann Educational Books (Asia) Ltd.

Panels that depict scenes from Buddhist literature are carved in the galleries of the Mendut temple on the island of Java (endpapers). Villagers go through their morning ablutions in the midst of dawn on the moody waters of Lake Jempang in Kalimantan on the island of Borneo (frontispiece). The magnificent Borobudur temple rises from the mists of Java, a monument to one of the glorious eras of the past (title page).

INDONESIA
Paradise · on · the · Equator

INDONESIA
Paradise · on · the · Equator

Photographed by
KAL MULLER

Written by
PAUL ZACH

Designed by
LEONARD LUERAS

Edited by
GRETCHEN LIU

TIMES EDITIONS

Contents

Paradise Found

*The Author introduces Himself and the Photographer to
the Reader, reveals their Motivations for producing this
Book and summarizes some of the complex Logistics of
their grueling Travels and Travails.*

A few months after arriving in Indonesia in 1978, I walked into the office of the press attaché at the American Embassy in Jakarta and announced that I had decided to stay for a while and freelance. The attaché was bidding farewell to another journalist, an American woman in her thirties whom he introduced with a flourish as Judy Bird Williams.

"I guess you'll be taking Judy's place then. She's decided to return to the States," the attaché told me. Then he smiled at Judy and added, "It's about time. She's been here eleven years." My jaw dropped. Several months in Central Java and Bali had certainly whetted my appetite for more of Indonesia. But at that point, 11 years seemed like an incomprehensibly long time to spend in the islands.

Now, more than eight years have passed — and I am still hopelessly hooked on Indonesia. I tried returning West to work in Florida and Jamaica. I could have settled in Hawaii. But I came back after a short time, resigned to the fact that Indonesia won't let go of me. And, frankly, I don't want it to.

Kal Muller, a photographer, scholar, linguist and tireless explorer, has found himself in much the same predicament. Awestruck by the wonders of Indonesia while photographing Bali in the early 1970s, Muller has since returned from his home in Mexico — a distance of about 19,000 kilometers — every year to continue exploring and photographing the islands. In the process, he has assembled a comprehensive photographic record of the classical aspects of contemporary Indonesia.

Kal and I first met at a party in Singapore in 1980. We were not surprised to learn that we had both fallen under the spell of the Indonesian islands. We found that at first we had been captivated by the obvious — the fragrant winds, the raw, natural beauty, the exotic cultures. But after we got to know each other better, we began to realize there was much more to our infatuation with these exquisite islands. In Indonesia, we had discovered a nation of people whose warmth and hospitality were genuine and whose unrelenting passion for life was invigorating and a source of creative inspiration.

Kal and I also realized we had a major investment in Indonesia. We had devoted some of the most critical years of our lives grappling with the daunting challenges of exploring the country. We had both weathered stormy seas and endless lazy tea-colored rivers aboard all manner of vessels, seaworthy and otherwise, crammed with people, farm produce and even sea turtles. We had flown through skies past smoking volcanic peaks floating above the clouds aboard Fokker Friendships and DC–10s, Indonesia-assembled Casa Aviocars, Twin Otters and Jumbo 747s, Puma and Bell helicopters, eight-seat Cessnas, Vicker Viscounts, spacious Airbuses and aging DC–3s, always counting on Garuda, the magic bird of Indonesian myth, and Bouraq, Muhammad's winged horse, to look after our airborne comfort and welfare.

We had survived stomach-churning rides in vintage Chevrolet Impalas, new Japanese cars and taxis, and whiplash-inducing spins around the hairpin curves of slippery mountain roads in *bemos* and *oplets*, hoping the 22 people crushed into the 10-passenger vehicle would cushion any sudden impact. We rode pillion over city sidewalks and solo over *padi* field dikes and jungle paths on motorcycles and wound through the bumpy back alleys of kampungs and villages in foot-propelled pedicabs. We rode on trains, clattering up-and-down moun-

After a dreamy dawn, women wearing wide-brimmed straw hats harvest rice on Bali (preceding pages); and during a balmy sunset, a man climbs a *lontar* tree on the island of Savu to collect sap used to brew *tuak*, a potent fermented palm wine that is a popular thirst-quencher throughout the vast archipelago.

tains through tunnels and across trestles suspended above wide gorges, our heads bouncing against windows, our arms and legs contorted into the corners of our seats, in vain attempts at sleep. I had scraped bloodsucking leeches from the soles of my feet in the jungles of Borneo, had been flattened by a tropical virus and unnerved by anxiety attacks. Kal had tangled with a rat that got caught in his hair while he was sleeping in Flores, suffered through bouts of malaria and stomach cramps. Indeed, sometimes it seemed that in our haste to get to paradise, we took some hair-raising detours through hell.

Still, we persevered. I wrapped myself in sarongs and put on headdresses to enter temples, then sweated through endless religious festivals and was nearly crushed by a mob of people at a parade of film stars in Yogyakarta. Kal scaled the towering masts of schooners, climbed trees and leaned out of the windows of helicopters and small planes, squinting through the viewfinder of his cameras. I carried my pens, pads, typewriters and tape recorders into traffic jams and jungles. Kal slung his tripod over his shoulder and lugged bags full of lenses and camera bodies up mountains and through swamps. Both of us suffered bouts of boredom, loneliness and frustration. Nothing is easy in Indonesia. But almost everything is rewarding. A single heady night lost in the perfumed embrace of the islands is intoxicating.

Somehow it didn't dawn on us until 1984 when we bumped into each other again in Singapore that all this could form the basis for a book. Although we had nearly two decades of Indonesia under our belts between the two of us, Kal and I decided to take another trip together. We spent five months in 1985 traveling through the archipelago.

Kal and I returned to Singapore, exhausted from our trip but exuberant. Then he sifted through 30,000 transparencies and I put some of our thoughts and experiences in writing. This volume is the result. It is our attempt to share our love for Indonesia, especially with all those who long ago abandoned their search for heaven on earth. Kal and I consider ourselves very fortunate. We found our paradise in these splendid islands on the equator.

Paul Zach
Singapore
March, 1987

A crew of whalers from the island of Lembata puts out to sea in a *peledang*, one of the many traditional handbuilt sailing vessels of Indonesia. Whaling without the unfair advantages of modern weapons and technology is still an honorable way of life in the culturally-rich Lesser Sundas, an island group in southeastern Indonesia.

The mountain of Suwela is fabulous and marvelous, everything tender and beautiful is here in abundance. I think it is the garden of Madana brought to earth to shatter the mind of one, who is overwhelmed by pangs of love as a result of living in separation from his beloved.

– from the Ramayana

The Nation

Passages about ancient Chinese Explorers, Marco Polo, lovestruck Dutch Sailors and contemporary Visitors who made Voyages to the Archipelago and raved about its Wonders presage a concise Survey of the Evolution, Ecology and History of the Islands.

Under azure skies and alabaster clouds, the islands of Indonesia cluster on the seductive seas of the equator. Caressed by the region's unusually gentle climate and nourished by the earth's fertile underbelly, the islands have spawned a profusion of unique flora and fauna and generated cultures that are so extraordinary they tax the imagination.

Pilgrims, explorers, intellectuals; adventurers and traders; writers and artists; people from every epoch and every corner of the earth have pursued their dreams only to find that they lead to the Indonesian archipelago. I-tsing, China's famous Buddhist globe-trotter, visited Sumatra in 671 A.D. and found such an important center of Mahayana education that he stayed for six months and learned Sanskrit before continuing on to India. Marco Polo, an Italian, was already numbed by China's amazing cornucopia when he discovered the wonders of the archipelago in the 13th century and wrote: "Pepper, nutmegs, spikenard, galangal, cubebs, cloves and all the other valuable spices and drugs ... the quantity of gold collected there exceeds all calculation and belief."

Young Dutch sailors, overwhelmed by the beauty, the warmth and the women of the islands, jumped ship in Bali in 1598, never to return home. Jan Pieterszoon Coen, another Dutchman, parlayed Indonesia's ambrosial spices into a colonial empire that lasted more than 300 years. The great 19th century British statesman, empire-builder, naturalist and sociologist, Sir Thomas Stamford Raffles, was so enthralled by the natural and cultural marvels of Java, he wrote massive volumes about them. Sir Alfred Russel Wallace, the prominent British naturalist, traveled 23,000 kilometers in eight years of exploring the archipelago and pronounced that it was composed of "the most luxuriant islands which adorn our earth's surface." Miguel Covarrubias, a Mexican painter, found inspiration in Bali's villages. And a young American anthropologist named Michael Rockefeller found fulfillment — and his fate — among the primitive tribes of Irian Jaya's swamps in 1961.

Inexplicably, Indonesia remains remarkably unknown in the modern world that lies outside its magical sphere. Only the Dutch, who long ruled it and whose fascination with the islands will never end, and the Australians, whose own vast landmass it overshadows, have any inkling of Indonesia's scope, boundaries and bounty. The archipelago is so obscure in most minds that Jonathan Swift figured no one would be the least bit suspicious if he used it as the locale for his islands of tiny people and giants, Lilliput and Brobdingnag, in *Gulliver's Travels*. More recently, movie mogul Dino de Laurentis figured that if an overgrown ape like King Kong actually lived anywhere, it had to be on an obscure island somewhere in the Indonesian chain.

The Indonesians themselves are acutely aware of the prevailing ignorance of their country. One of its most perceptive writers, Umar Kayam, sketched a scene in one of his short stories set in Manhattan in which his wife good-naturedly indulges the bewilderment of a European acquaintance:

"Vere iz your country?"

"Indonesia."

"Ah yez, yez. Near Siam, no?"

"No, I'm sorry. You must be thinking of Indochina. People always confuse the two."

"Aaah, Indo ... h-Indo ... "

"Indonesia."

Indelible images from a nation of islands (preceding pages): simmering Mt. Merapi, Central Java's "Fire Mountain" and a Borobudur Buddha; the schooners of South Sulawesi's Bugis people docked in Jakarta and thousands of Muslims prostrate in prayer in the capital's grand Istiqlal Mosque; and a woman on Lombok (left) planting rice, the food staple of Indonesian life.

"Aah, h-Indo-nesia. Let me guess vere it iz."

My wife nodded, smiling. It was the nod of a confirmed card player, convinced her cards were good.

"Eh, near Korea?"

"Too far north, Madame."

My own recollection of anything remotely connected with Indonesia was an old Pan Am Airlines board game that I played as a youngster. The roll of the dice often brought my plastic airplane to a landing in a city referred to back in those days by the old Dutch spelling as *Djakarta*. Of course I hadn't the vaguest idea that the city was the capital of a nation called Indonesia and I certainly had no notion that some day a real Pan American jumbo jet would not only take me to Jakarta, but that I would eventually take up residence there.

In 1977, at the age of 26, I was one of four journalists in the United States awarded a Gannett Fellowship in Asian Studies at the University of Hawaii. I resigned from my job as a reporter for a Florida newspaper determined to use the fellowship program as a stepping stone to a post as a foreign correspondent in Asia. In my application for the program I had proposed to focus my studies on Southeast Asia in general. But the astute curator of the Gannett Fellowships, Windsor G. Hackler, a retired diplomat who had served at the U.S. Embassy in Jakarta, convinced me I should concentrate on Indonesia.

First, I took a course in the Indonesian language. For five hours a day, five days a week in a classroom on the Manoa Valley campus of the University of Hawaii, I immersed myself in the language and culture of Indonesia. The teacher, a young Javanese man, spent an inordinate amount of time romancing us with stories about Bali, Java and Sumatra, about the epic mythology of the *Ramayana*, the Asian equivalent of the Greek Odyssey, about fabulous ancient temples and palaces and awesome rituals, about rajahs and sultans and the hospitality of the island peoples, and, of particular interest to a young bachelor, the natural beauty of Indonesia's women. Hawaii was nice, but Indonesia sounded better.

After completing the year-long fellowship, I joined a study tour of the Far East. The last stop on the itinerary was the island of Bali. Never before had I

Indonesians call their country *Tanah Air Kita*, "Our Land and Water." Here, typical scenes: at sea (top) fishermen use handcrafted vessels and nets off Padang on Sumatra's west coast; and on land (bottom) a man keeps warm high up the slopes of the volcanic caldera around brooding Mt. Bromo in East Java.

The Republic of Indonesia encompasses the world's largest archipelago boasting more than 13,677 islands in all. Under alabaster clouds and against the azure equatorial seas, Komodo Island in the Lesser Sundas group looks alluring and reveals no hint that it is the abode of vicious, meat-eating "dragons."

seen such colors, witnessed such ritual, inhaled such fragrances or felt so at home so far away from home. The rest of the group returned to the security of their homes in Honolulu. I stayed behind, intrigued by the prospect of what the future might hold.

During the years I have lived and traveled in Indonesia, I have most enjoyed seeing it the way the earliest inhabitants and explorers did — by sea. I covered thousands of kilometers and spent many weeks aboard every kind of vessel that has probably ever traveled in Indonesian waters, paddling up coffee-colored rivers in a dugout canoe, bucking sapphire seas aboard a Bugis-built *pinisi* schooner, gliding across aqua lagoons above gaudy coral gardens in a sleek outrigger, steaming through black oceans under a moody sky swept by smoky clouds on the deck of an enormous passenger vessel, always coming ashore on another verdant island.

It is the most rewarding way to travel through Indonesia and the most appropriate. For of Indonesia's total area of more than five million square kilometers, three-quarters is water. Even though the archipelago is the world's largest, boasting 13,677 islands, it is possible to travel for days across vast expanses of water, kicking up flying fish and trailing schools of frolicking pilot whales or dolphins, without spotting land. The Pacific and Indian Oceans; the South China Sea; the Sunda and Sumba and Makassar Straits; the Java, Flores, Arafura, Banda and Timor Seas; countless lakes, rivers, harbors, bays and inlets; an infinite number of bodies of waters swirl in and around the islands.

Splashed across 5,120 kilometers of equatorial seas from end to end, the mighty Indonesian archipelago girds the earth's waistline for nearly one-eighth of its entire circumference, further than the distance from San Francisco on the Pacific Ocean to Bermuda in the Atlantic or from Rome to Karachi in Pakistan. Indonesia's westernmost city, Sabang on Weh Island, lies a few hundred kilometers west of southern Thailand. The nation's eastern point is Merauke in Irian Jaya, at almost the same latitude as Adelaide, Australia.

There are 30 smaller archipelagos in the large one, grouped into four geographic entities: the Greater Sundas, which include Sumatra, Java, Sulawesi and Borneo; the Lesser Sundas, which stretch from Bali to Timor; the Moluccas, a sprawl of about a thousand islands that includes Ambon, Ternate, Tidore, the Bandas, Arus, Tanimbars, Halmahera and Morotai; and Irian Jaya, the western portion of New Guinea and adjacent islands.

As islands go, some of Indonesia's rank among the world's largest. Sumatra is over 288,000 square kilometers making it roughly as big as all of Spain. Java is 81,920 square kilometers of fuming volcanic ranges and dazzling coastal seascapes. Spider-shaped Sulawesi encompasses 227,654 square kilometers. Of Borneo, the world's third largest island at 740,000 square kilometers, almost three-quarters is the Indonesian territory of Kalimantan; and of New Guinea, second most massive after Greenland with a total of 773,000 square kilometers, nearly half is the Indonesian territory of Irian Jaya which makes that province alone the size of Japan.

The easternmost islands of the Irian area are part of the Australian continental mass known as the Sahul shelf. The northwestern islands are the exposed summits of the submerged Sunda shelf, once part of the Asian continent. In fact, geologists believe the Greater Sundas and part of the Lesser Sundas were not an archipelago at all during the Mesozoic era, but merely a peninsular extension of Southeast Asia, a theory substantiated by the unusually shallow seas in the area.

Violent upheavals in the earth's crust some 60 million years ago pushed up two parallel arcs of mountain ridges. One, although mostly underwater, exhibits some of its highest peaks in the small island chains south and west of Sumatra and further east in Sumba, Timor, the Tanimbars, Ceram and Buru. The more pronounced of the two ranges is responsible for the shapely contours of Sumatra, Java, Bali, Lombok, Sumbawa and Flores. When the great glaciers of the Ice Age began to melt, some of the lowlands of these ridges were submerged and the modern Indonesian archipelago took shape. Sudden, temperamental convulsions continue to mold the existing islands and push up new ones today.

Indeed, the most spectacular feature of Indonesia's islands are the volcanos, which have been both a bane and a blessing to their inhabitants. They have not only scarred the landscapes and snuffed out plant, animal and human life, but they have disgorged some of the earth's most fertile soils. Less

Mighty volcanos shaped the dramatic landscapes of Indonesia and continue to do so today. Indeed, in the Sunda Straits between Sumatra and Java where the mighty Krakatau volcano vanished in a thunderous explosion that shook the entire world in 1883, grows a new island nourished by ongoing eruptions. Indonesians call the temperamental young island Anak Krakatau, the "child of Krakatau."

than a century after Krakatau volcano rocked the earth with one of history's most violent explosions in 1883, its remnants, Rakata and Sertung islands, were alive with birds and other fauna. Life has returned to other areas devastated by that eruption, too.

Vulcanologists have identified 128 active craters among Indonesia's 500 volcanos. Of the 221 volcanos in the world that have been identified as dangerous by the international Volcanic Explosiveness Indicator, 37 are in Indonesia. At the top of that volatile list is Tambora on the island of Sumbawa. Tiny Ternate and Tidore in the Moluccas are little more than smouldering volcanic peaks.

More than 170,000 people have perished since the 16th century as a result of volcanic eruptions. Storms of debris from an eruption of West Java's Mt. Galunggung in 1982, blanketed Bandung and other towns in the area with five centimeters of ash and nearly brought down two Boeing 747 jumbo jets filled with passengers. An estimated 500 to 1,000 tremors, most of them minor, activate seismographs from somewhere in the archipelago each year. While such activity has touched off destructive tidal waves, earthquakes are generally mild.

Many of Indonesia's people live their entire lives in the shadows of volcanos. They have worshiped and respected the restless mountains since the days when their ancestors believed that eruptions were mighty temper tantrums thrown by the gods.

The Tenggerese of East Java pay homage each year to the Supreme Lord Sanghyang Widi Wasa who is believed to inhabit the bleak wastes of the Tengger massif. There, during the feast of Kesada, thousands of pilgrims recite mantras and throw live poultry, money, flower petals and other offerings into the gaping abyss of Mt. Bromo, a modification of ancient ceremonies when they pitched human sacrifices into the crater. The Tenggerese also bury their dead with their heads towards an adjoining volcano, Semeru, Java's tallest peak.

The volcanos are the fountainheads of some of the most dramatic and ethereal terrain in the world. Verdigris peaks, storybook waterfalls, jagged coralline outcroppings, ravines ravished by rushing rivers, carpets of rain forest, lowland swamps and savannas, stark deserts and coastlines fringed with white, golden and black sand beaches and mangrove thickets merge into surrealistic landscapes that

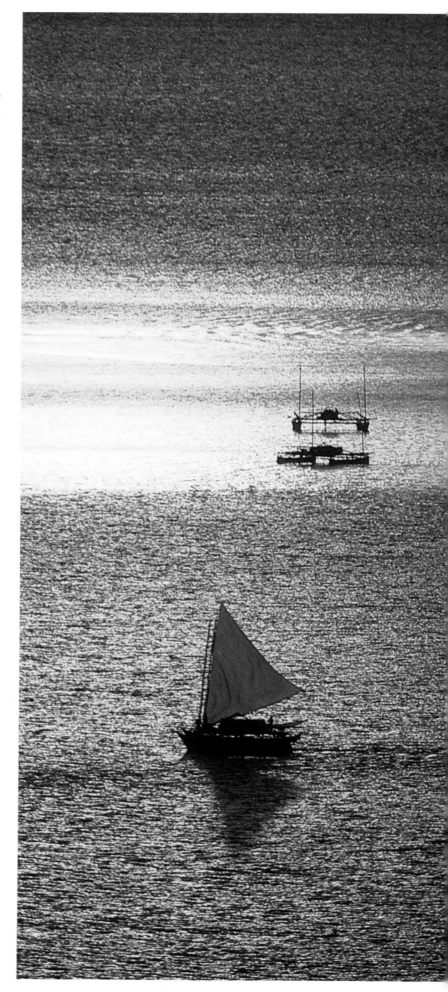

Except for monsoon rains and equatorial heat, Indonesia's climate is relatively gentle. Most of the time, its winds are soothing and its seas halcyon. Burnished by the golden rays of the setting sun, the sea off the coast of Flores provides smooth sailing for the catamarans and *bagan* traps of the island's fishermen.

Sultry skies, foamy seas, majestic coconut palms and a carpet of
maturing rice make for a typical pastoral scene (top) along Java's
west coast, while delicate ferns (bottom) grace the lush tropical
rain forests inland on Java and other Indonesian islands.

provide appropriate backdrops for some of the mystical rites of the diverse cultures.

Indonesia is as rich in resources as it is beautiful. Oil, natural gas, copper, nickel, tin, coal, phosphate and other minerals are mined for export and domestic use. The vast forests yield lumber and rattan. Rice, rubber, palm oil, sugar cane, coffee, tea, coconuts, cloves, nutmeg and other agricultural products flourish in the fertile soils. The seas, too, are a source of nourishment.

Although the Indonesian islands all lie within six latitudinal degrees north and 11 degrees south of the equator, there are considerable variations in climate. For the most part, it is hot and humid, although not always unpleasantly so, at lower altitudes where most of the population lives. But in the higher elevations of Java, Sulawesi and Sumatra, temperatures dip sharply and the air is even damper. The variety of vegetation also changes at higher elevations. Tropical palms and ferns give way to firs and montane forests. Several of the peaks of Irian Jaya's majestic midsection rise to about 5,000 meters, are devoid of life and are perpetually crowned with glistening sheets of snow and ice.

The greater Jakarta metropolitan area is a good barometer of typical climatic conditions. The city's thermometers rarely exceed 32 degrees centigrade or fall below 23 degrees. But just 100 kilometers southeast of the capital, the pleasant Puncak resort area at the 1,200 meter level enjoys cool nights year-round. Indonesians have only two names for the seasons of the year, *musim hujan* and *musim kering* — wet and dry respectively. These seasons are governed by the west monsoon which brings months of regular heavy rain to Sumatra, Java and the Lesser Sundas from November to around March and the weaker east monsoon that blows in drier Australian air the rest of the year. About half the country gets 190 to 315 centimeters of rainfall annually.

The contrast between the wet and dry seasons is more apparent in the islands of the Lesser Sundas than it is in Java and Sumatra, however. And because the east monsoon picks up increasing amounts of moisture as it moves across the Arafura Sea, parts of the Moluccas and Irian Jaya tend to be wetter from May to August and drier during the winter. Heavy rains combine with erosion to produce damaging floods at times, but severe weather of any sort is rare. The typhoons that plague the China coast, Hong Kong, Japan and the Philippines usually spare Indonesia's islands. On the contrary, Indonesian winds are gentle, invigorating the body and soothing the senses.

Woodlands blanket about 60 per cent of Indonesia. There are more than 113 million hectares of rain forest (only Brazil has more) filled with an incredible variety of plants and an equally unfathomable array of animals and insects. Two distinct categories of flora and fauna are roughly separated by the Wallace Line, a somewhat indistinct boundary along the edge of the shallow Sunda shelf between Borneo and Sulawesi and Bali and Lombok, named after the British naturalist who identified it. West of the Wallace Line, on Borneo, Java, Sumatra and Bali, are apes and monkeys, jungle cats, rhinos and elephants, wild cattle and multi-layered rain forests dripping with lianas, epiphytes and colorful flowers common to continental South Asia. East of the line on Sulawesi, the Moluccas, Irian Jaya, and Lesser Sundas are the kind of radically different eucalyptus, casuarina, grassy savannas and the kangaroos, wombats, opposums and other marsupials peculiar to the Australian outback.

At least 40,000 species of plants and trees, ten per cent of all those in the world, have been identified in the archipelago. Among them are the bizarre Rafflesia, found almost exclusively in the province of Bengkulu in Sumatra. Its petal spread of one meter makes it the world's largest flower. Bougainvillea, fragrant frangipani and jasmine; infinite species of orchids; and exotic fruits including the spiky durian, hairy rambutan, snake-skinned salak, hard shelled mangosteen and bananas of all shapes and sizes also flourish. There are 3,000 kinds of trees in the mighty rain forests of Sumatra and Kalimantan and, by some estimates, Borneo alone boasts twice as many species of trees as all of Africa. Hardwoods like the awesome meranti trees provide a leafy umbrella up to 60 meters high, so dense in spots that sunlight never penetrates to the ground in the deepest jungles. Other dipterocarps, bamboo, sago and some 150 species of palm trees, thrive.

Perhaps the most popular of the archipelago's denizens is the orangutan. In fact, its name is composed of two Indonesian words that translate as "man of the forest." Once prevalent in many parts of

Indonesia's islands have spawned creatures that are among the rarest, oddest and most magnificent on earth. At left, the regal armor-plated rhinoceros, elegant Sumatran tiger and the beloved orangutan, literally "man of the forest," of Borneo and Sumatra. Above, the Komodo dragons of the Lesser Sundas, hardy survivors of the dinosaur age.

Indonesia, the endangered orangutan now lives in the wild mainly in protected preserves in Kalimantan and Sumatra. Herds of elephants still roam in Sumatra, occasionally running afoul of farmers. In 1985, a combined force of 375 helicopter-borne soldiers and police, assisted by hundreds of residents on foot, rounded up about 70 elephants that had raided and pillaged farms in Aceh. The pachyderms were relocated in the 950,000-hectare Gunung Leuser National Park. Such incidents prompted the government to set up an elephant training center in Lampung in an effort to funnel the animal's energies into constructive uses.

Monkeys are found in such great numbers that they also prove to be a nuisance. However, the rhinoceros apparently have disappeared from Borneo and are in danger of extinction in Sumatra and Java. And only 600 tigers are still believed to exist on Sumatra and Java. They are far outnumbered by the wily leopard. Some 200 species of snakes slither on land and in the waters including the deadly banded krait and taipan. Reticulated pythons that grow up to 11 meters have been known to swallow wild boars and humans — whole. Irian Jaya has enormous tree-climbing rats and 10-meter long crocodiles. Legions of cockroaches, bats, mosquitoes, ants, rats and gecko and tokay lizards are found almost everywhere. A team of 125 scientists from 18 countries spent several months in the Bone-Dumoga National Park of Sulawesi in 1985 and identified at least 10,000 new species of insects.

Bird life is also present in profusion. On one of our expeditions, Kal and I came across a dedicated group of birdwatchers led by David Bishop, a biological consultant from London and Ben King, one of the authors of the definitive field guide to the birds of Southeast Asia. Bishop, who has spent years studying wildlife in Indonesia, holds the distinction of having rediscovered one species of the country's revered bird of paradise previously believed to be extinct — Wallace's standard-wing — in the jungles of Halmahera Island, an accomplishment that attracted a documentary television crew from the BBC.

According to Bishop, 1,627 of the world's 9,000 species of birds are native to Indonesia. "There are more kinds of birds here than anywhere other than perhaps South America. There's a lot of activity out there," he told us while keeping his eyes glued to his Leitz binoculars. Just then a Christmas Island frigate bird glided above the ship. "This is absolutely incredible," Bishop shouted as he and his fellow birders strained their eyes. King, who claims he has seen more birds in Asia than anyone else has, said that in the course of visiting Halmahera, Sulawesi and Java during the preceding month, he had spotted 100 species he had never seen before.

King, Bishop and other naturalists, both foreign and Indonesian, whom we encountered during our travels, expressed concern that the demands of development are destroying the habitats of increasingly rare flora and fauna in many of the countries of Southeast Asia, including Indonesia. But some commended the Indonesian government for its conservation efforts. More than 300 nature reserves, national parks and protected forest areas have been designated by the government encompassing 6.5 per cent of the country's total land area.

Before his death in 1980, the first Vice President of the Republic of Indonesia, Dr. Mohammad Hatta, gave an extensive interview in which he touched on the significance of the name he and the other founders gave their nation. "Choosing the name Indonesia for our archipelago ... was in fact a reflection of an attitude of unity, a unity of soul and spirit, of the generation of the vanguards and pioneers of Indonesian independence."

The forging of a unified nation from the incredibly diverse collection of cultures is one of the remarkable stories of the 20th century. But the bonds between many of the islands hark back almost to their earliest civilizations.

Inscriptions among the earliest found in all of Southeast Asia indicate sophisticated communities existed in Borneo as long ago as 400 A.D. and in Java around 450 A.D. The Prasasti Tugu, a boulder excavated from Kampung Batu Tumbuh near Jakarta's Tanjung Priok port is inscribed with *wenggi* characters of South India's fifth century Pallava Dynasty. The words tell of "a beautiful river of pure water," probably referring to the Citarum. The beauty of the river has since been marred by the demands of the dense population, but it still flows east of Jakarta. Other inscribed stones found in the area similar to the *Prasasti Tugu* reveal that a king named Purnawarman ruled over a kingdom called

Some of man's earliest ancestors have left their mark in parts of the Indonesian archipelago. The oldest relics were drawings carved in stone that were discovered along the banks of the Mahakam River in East Kalimantan and possibly made by ancestors of the Dayak who carved this wooden totem (right).

Taruma which may have had its seat near Bekasi, not far from the nation's contemporary capital. He appears to have engineered the construction of a canal system on the flat, flood-prone coastal plains. The Indian script and stone statues of Hindu deities also found in the area suggest that Taruma had established international relations.

The notebooks of Buddhist wayfarers like Fa Hsien indicate that Java and Sumatra also developed early trade links with China. In fact, Indonesia is the only place in the world outside China where ceramics of the Han Dynasty (206 B.C. to 220 A.D) have been unearthed. In his classic *History of Southeast Asia*, D.G.E. Hall concludes:

> "By the beginning of the seventh century the outlines of Indonesian history (were) beginning to become apparent. A harbor kingdom was well established on the southeast coast of Sumatra and there were several important kingdoms on the island of Java. Expanding Indonesian communications with the outside world were bringing wealth and new ideas to that region. It is not surprising that the following centuries were to see the rise of substantial empires and a flowering civilization in western Indonesia."

The first powerful Indonesian empire, Srivijaya, emerged in the seventh century in the vicinity of Palembang in Sumatra, nourished by increasing maritime trade with China, India and other countries. Its predominant religion was Mahayana Buddhism. Srivijaya conquered the island's other states, Malayu and Banka, and extended its sphere of influence to Java and the Malay Peninsula. The need to communicate even then was giving rise to the use of Malay as a kind of regional Esperanto.

Meanwhile, Central Java was the domain of the Hindu dynasty of Mataram. During the middle of the eighth century, King Sanjaya of Mataram controlled Bali, West Java and parts of Sumatra. But in a sudden change of fortunes that historical scholars are unable to explain, another line of Buddhist rulers, the Sailendras, rose to prominence about 760 A.D. The Dutch geologist R.W. van Bemmelen suggests that Mataram may have been the victim of an eruption of Mt. Merapi in 1006, a theory supported by an inscription found on the Calcutta Stone that described the disappearance of the kingdom "in a milky sea." The Sailendras allied themselves with Srivijaya's leaders, foreshadowing latter-day links between the islands.

Whatever the fate of King Sanjaya and Mataram, the clashing political and religious ideologies in the islands and rapid shifts of power sparked an outburst of artistic expression that produced some of the world's greatest monuments. In an apparent effort to overshadow temples built by Sanjaya on the Dieng Plateau to honor the Hindu deity Siva, the Sailendras constructed the Borobudur, the immense Buddhist *stupa*, above the Kedu Plain in Central Java. Containing more than 400 stone statues of the Buddha, an estimated 50,000 sculptors, stone-carvers, masons and laborers worked from 778 to 856 A.D. to erect the edifice. Numerous smaller Buddhist temples also adorn Central Java, an enduring testimony to the architectural achievements of the Sailendras. Conversely, rulers loyal to vanquished Mataram managed to regain a foothold in the east. They responded with more Hindu shrines, notably the vast Prambanan temple complex of 156 monuments and eight major temples on the Opak River near Surakarta that was built in the 10th century. Literature, dance and music also flourished.

The Sailendras' Srivijaya empire, racked by internal feuding and besieged by the renewed strength of the Hindus in East Java, soon began to crumble into small fiefdoms. Airlangga, a king of Javanese and Balinese descent, managed to restore some order in the 11th century. The classic Javanese epic, the *Mahabarata*, is loosely based on Airlangga's exploits and provides the fodder for the *wayang kulit* – shadow puppet – dramas. Airlangga established his power base in Kediri in East Java, controlled Bali and Ternate and strengthened trade ties with Sumatra and Borneo. Kediri lost out to another East Java kingdom, Singosari, in 1222 A.D. Its last ruler, Kertanegara, presided over a marriage of the Hindu and Buddhist religious factions.

Power shifted to Majapahit around 1293 when its first king, Vijaya, succeeded in driving Kubla Khan's invading Mongol warriors from Java. The rise of the Majapahit empire was a turning point in the evolution of a unified Indonesian state. Some historians believe that its most vaunted leader, Hayam Wuruk, and his chief minister Gajah

Sophisticated civilizations that were highly-developed and infinitely creative — like those of Srivijaya and Majapahit — ruled ancient Indonesia. The legacy of their glorious eras is written in old and new artifacts and art like the myriad temples of Central and East Java with their facades of grimacing gods.

Dockworkers unload flour from Sumatra at Merak on Java's west coast. The harbor is bustling with an almost constant flow of cargo ships and ferry boats between the two big islands. Agricultural commodities have been a mainstay of the Indonesian economy since colonial times when the Dutch shipped lucrative cargoes of spices back to Europe.

Mada, managed to bring most of the islands that make up the contemporary republic under their jurisdiction, from Bangka, Belitung and south eastern Sumatra, to the Anambas and Natunas islands off the west coast of Borneo, parts of Kalimantan, most of Java, Madura, Bali, eastern Timor, some of south Sulawesi, and even parts of Ceram, Halmahera and Irian Jaya. Beyond the archipelago, Majapahit's influence extended to the Malay Peninsula and an island at its southern tip that was to become Singapore, and to Cambodia, Siam, Champa, Vietnam and the Philippines. A study by Indonesian scholar Slametmuljana revealed that even the emperors of China's Ming Dynasty respected the might of Majapahit. Slametmuljana noted that Gajah Mada announced his political program before the Queen and high officials of the empire. It was called *sumpah nusantara*, the "vow to conquer the lands beyond Java." To this day *nusantara* is the word Indonesians use for "archipelago" and "fatherland."

A British historian, M.C. Ricklefs, described the capital of Majapahit, located in the Brantas Valley about 48 kilometers southeast of modern Surabaya, as a "grand affair, with great annual festivities" where both Buddhism and Hinduism were practiced. "The memory of Majapahit's greatness has lived on in Indonesia, and it is sometimes seen as establishing a precedent for the present political boundaries of the Republic," Ricklefs wrote.

The reign of the Majapahit kings also saw the rise of another important influence in the islands, Islam. Although Muslim gravestones from the 11th century have been discovered in East Java, it was Marco Polo, after a stopover in Sumatra in 1292, who revealed in his writings that in the Sumatran kingdom of Perlac "those who dwell in the seaport towns have been converted to the religion of Mahomet, by the Saracen merchants who constantly frequent them." A sultan named Malik as-Salih ruled North Sumatra from Samudra until his death in 1297. Ricklefs said tombstones found in East Java suggest that some members of the island's elite adopted Islam when Majapahit was at the height of its glory.

Following the death of Gajah Mada in 1364 and Hayam Wuruk in 1389, Majapahit declined almost as quickly as it had emerged. The peninsula-based kingdom of Malacca, whose ruler converted to Islam around 1400, filled the power vacuum in central Sumatra. The Islamic state of Demak began flexing its muscles in East Java and, by the beginning of the 16th century, Aceh and its fervent Muslims were expanding their influence in northern Sumatra. That century brought another presence to the archipelago – the Europeans.

Jacob Manuhutu scratched his ebony black hair and surveyed the impossible shades of blues and greens — indigo, mazarine, cerulean, aquamarine, — that dye the waters around Saparua and other islands in the Moluccas. Around us, the charcoal gray walls of Fort Duurstede stood in stark contrast to the blinding tropical colors. There seemed to be some confusion between Jacob, one of the island's village heads, and his colleagues about the origin of the well-preserved fortification. "We had the Portugese for 10 years, the Dutch for 350 and the Japanese for three years," he said and left it at that.

Crumbling forts like the one in Saparua, the relics of Western colonization, clutter the Indonesian archipelago. The Portuguese began building them after they conquered Malacca in 1511, then sent their armadas to the Moluccas. These paradisiacal lands were known to the European world as the "Spice Islands" because they were laden with nutmegs, cloves, mace, pepper and other prized seasonings. The Portuguese allied themselves with the ruling family of Ternate and began shipping the valuable spices back to Europe via Malacca. Portugal's presence in the archipelago was brief, but influential. The Portuguese built a string of forts from North Sumatra to Sunda Kelapa, around which modern Jakarta grew; in Sulawesi; through Tidore, Ambon, Banda and other islands in the Moluccas; and in Flores and Timor in the Lesser Sundas. In fact, the Portuguese maintained sovereignty over East Timor until the colony was integrated into the Republic in 1975. Other enduring reminders include Christian names like Manahutu's, pockets of Catholicism, and Portuguese words like *meja* for table, *sepatu* for shoe, *mentega* for butter, *pesta* for party, and *bola* for ball.

Portuguese power in the archipelago waned at the turn of the 17th century. In moved the Dutch warrior merchants. The government of the Netherlands granted a charter to the VOC, the United East

Women have always played key roles in the history and development of Indonesia. Raden Ajeng Kartini, a Javanese princess who eloquently argued for emancipation long before the "women's liberation movement" of the West, and Christina Martha Tiahahu, a leader of a 19th century revolt against the Dutch in Ambon, are only two of the heroines who are revered ancestors of this solemn gathering of village women.

India Company, in 1602. By 1610, the company's warships were muscling into trade in Ambon, Ternate, Tidore, the Bandas and Sumatra. The foundations of Dutch dominance were laid when the increasingly important settlement at Sunda Kelapa, then called Jayakarta, was seized in 1619. The colony's first governor-general, Jan Pieterszoon Coen, rebuilt it along the lines of a typical town in Holland and renamed it Batavia, after an ancient Germanic region and tribe of Flanders.

With Batavia as its base, the VOC, also known as the Jan Compagnie, forged the most lucrative mercantile empire of the time, a superpower that eventually encompassed parts of the world as far flung as Africa and Japan and included most of modern Indonesia. British scholar C.R. Boxer wrote:

> "Small but obstinate nuclei of Portuguese missionaries and traders remained in Timor, Solor and Flores (Larantuka); but they were merely a local nuisance and not a threat to the expanding power of the VOC elsewhere in Indonesia. The VOC in 1664 was a colossal organization, comparable to one of the modern great multinational firms, when due allowance is made for differences in time, space and demography."

Meanwhile, the baton of local power in Central Java passed back to Mataram during the colorful reign of the charismatic Sultan Agung, 1613–45. His rule, based in Yogyakarta, was the pinnacle of the resilient old dynasty. Sultan Agung made a valiant but vain attempt to drive the Dutch from Batavia. Dutch exploitation of the islands produced ruthless episodes, like Coen's wholesale slaughter of people in the Moluccas in the 1620s, and the Dutch interfered in the affairs of local ruling elites throughout the archipelago whenever it was deemed necessary to maintain or enhance their commercial hegemony. But the leaders of Aceh, the states of Gowa and Bone in South Sulawesi, and the sultans of Ternate and Tidore maintained some power. They occasionally entered into uneasy alliances with the Dutch and against them or with and against each other and just as often fought among themselves. In Java, VOC meddling and internal squabbling led to the disintegration of the Mataram empire. It splintered into separate courts in Yogyakarta and Solo (Surakarta) in the 1700s.

Exhausted by warring, inefficiency, corruption and a decline in demand for Moluccan spices, the VOC went bankrupt in 1800. The Dutch government assumed administrative responsibility for the East Indies until the Napoleonic Wars in Europe transferred control to the British in 1811. Indonesia enjoyed a more enlightened form of leadership under Lieutenant-Governor Thomas Stamford Raffles, but the British sojourn lasted only five years. In that time Raffles implemented some administrative reforms that improved the lot of the Javanese peasants, traveled extensively and wrote his classic, *The History of Java*.

When the Dutch returned, they found the people of the archipelago were simmering with resentment against European domination of their islands. Prince Diponegoro, son of the sultan of Yogyakarta and a paramount hero of Indonesian history, led an unsuccessful rebellion against the Dutch that lasted from 1825 to 1830. More than 200,000 Javanese and 15,000 Dutch soldiers and civilians died from the fighting, disease and starvation. Harsher administrative policies resulted, most notably the hated Dutch *cultuurstelsel*, or cultivation system, which required each village to use a portion of its land solely for the production of export crops like coffee, sugar, tea, tobacco, indigo and spices for sale at fixed prices to the colonial government. The policy reduced many farmers to virtual slaves while enriching corrupt Indonesian and Dutch officials and Chinese entrepreneurs. The novel *Max Havelaar*, written by a crusading Dutchman, brought the horrors of the system home to the Netherlands in the 1860s and turned public opinion against it, but the system was dismantled slowly and persisted into the 20th century.

To its credit, the colonial administration installed railway lines and postal and telegraph systems, improved harbor facilities and implemented other development projects that eliminated some of the communication barriers between the peoples of the islands. However, the projects more often than not were motivated more by the needs of the economy of the Netherlands than out of concern for the welfare of the island peoples. The Dutch continued to use military force to subdue stubbornly independent regimes and the occasional rebellion.

By the time the Dutch began toying with a new "enlightened policy" toward its colony at the beginning of the 20th century, a growing number of Indonesian aristocrats and intellectuals had begun organizing themselves into nationalistic groups. Muslim groups like Muhammadiyah and Sarekat Islam also agitated for a voice in the system.

In 1926, a charismatic man of Javanese and Balinese parentage helped found the Indonesian National Party, PNI. His name was Sukarno. He shook the very foundations of the colony with his powerful rhetoric and sizzling speeches. Most importantly, he called on the diverse groups in the archipelago to unite to rid the islands of Dutch tyranny. In Holland itself, Indonesian students like Mohammad Hatta and Sutan Sjahrir began agitating for an end to Dutch rule. The Dutch jailed or exiled the men several times. But they continued to agitate for an Indonesian voice in government.

The "rising sun" of the Japanese unwittingly accelerated the dawn of independence in Indonesia. Japanese armies swept through Asia and marched into the archipelago in 1942. Although the occupation was brutal, the Japanese mounted an anti-Western campaign that helped crystallize Indonesian sentiment against Dutch rule. They also permitted the formation of a political movement headed by Sukarno and Hatta and helped create a crack

Indonesian army schooled in guerrilla tactics.

During a visit to Banda Neira, where her husband had been exiled along with Hatta, I spoke with the wife of the late Sutan Sjahrir about Indonesia's ambivalent attitude toward the Japanese occupation. "Only during the Japanese occupation did we come back to our own culture," Mrs. Sjahrir said. "One positive effect was that we were required to learn either the Japanese or Indonesian language. The Dutch never bothered to teach us our own language."

When the Japanese surrendered to the Allied Forces in 1945, Sukarno read a statement signed by himself and Hatta from the porch of his house in Jakarta. The date was August 17. The document proclaimed the independence of Indonesia.

On the southeast outskirts of Jakarta stands an impressive monument called Pancasila Sakti. It commemorates an idealistic concept propounded by Sukarno that has guided Indonesia since he declared independence: belief in a sovereign state, one god, representative government, social justice and respect for human values. The striking statues and reliefs also recall the turbulent times the new nation experienced during its first 25 years as an independent republic struggling to remain united.

When the Japanese left the Indonesian islands

From prehistoric times to the modern war of independence, the men of most Indonesian islands have been fearless warriors. Fired by their ancient customs, men such as these from Timor (above left) and Nias (above right) still maintain traditional techniques of combat, at least ceremonially.

Displays of national and cultural pride occur regularly throughout the immense archipelago. A group of Dayaks representing one of the remote upriver villages in East Kalimantan (top) parade wearing their traditional festive dress of bird feathers. A majorette (bottom) and boy scouts (top right) march in contemporary uniforms indicative of lingering colonial influences.

after World War II, the Dutch promptly returned and tried to restore their authority and a full-fledged revolutionary war broke out. It wasn't until 1949 after years of bloody skirmishing that world opinion and American pressure convinced the Netherlands to recognize Indonesian sovereignty over all the archipelago except western New Guinea. Bung Karno, "Brother," as the Indonesians called their popular leader, became the republic's first President and Hatta was appointed its first Vice President.

Sukarno's greatest accomplishment was the establishment of a unified national identity among many of the diverse peoples of the archipelago and a strong central government. He fostered the use of *Bahasa Indonesia* as the common medium of communication in islands that were a babel of more than 300 languages. In international arenas, Sukarno proved that people who had for so long suffered under colonial domination could stand on an equal footing with the developed Western world. The Dutch presence in the region came to a total end in 1963 when, after years of political posturing and several military clashes, the United Nations transferred sovereignty of western New Guinea to Indonesia.

The euphoria of independence was soon dampened by reality. The task of rallying all of the diverse groups in the island behind the red-and-

white flag of a single government system proved more formidable than Sukarno anticipated. He had to use military force to suppress rebellious outbreaks in Aceh, West Sumatra and North Sulawesi. His campaign of confrontation against Malaysia and its proposed federation of states proved nearly disastrous and alienated him from the rulers of neighboring countries. Sukarno's personal behavior also became increasingly erratic. He was criticized for his flagrant womanizing and extravagant lifestyle. He also lavished public funds on questionable projects at the expense of the fragile economy.

Sukarno's biggest error was in misjudging the rise of the PKI, Indonesia's Communist party, and in aligning himself with Communist China and its satellites. Buoyed by their growing influence, the PKI attempted to overthrow Indonesia's constitutional government on the night of September 30, 1965, a year Sukarno had prophetically proclaimed "the year of living dangerously." The gruesome events which lasted into the following morning climaxed at the "crocodile hole," the well where the Pancasila Sakti monument is located. Seven military officers, six of them generals, were killed in the coup attempt. Their bodies were stuffed down the well, after they had been tortured and murdered by young women who were members of left-wing groups. Quick action by a young general named Suharto snuffed out the rebellion. But its repercussions resulted in the most tragic episode in Indonesian history. During months that came to be known as the "night of the long knives," tens of thousands of people, many of them Communists or their sympathizers, were reported to have been killed in reprisals that followed. During the chaos Sukarno lost his grip on the government. He died in 1970, still revered as one of the nation's founding fathers.

Suharto's hard line against the Communists and other agitators eventually restored order. He officially took over as President in 1968 and established a government known as the "New Order." It inherited an unwieldy country on the brink of economic and social collapse. Those things considered, Suharto's record in restoring peace, order and hope has been remarkable. Boosted by exports of natural resources, particularly oil, a bright corps of ministers has put the country on a relatively sound economic footing. Indonesia surprised the world by

An honor guard, in flawlessly white uniforms trimmed with red, is put through its paces at Istana Merdeka, the Freedom Palace, in Central Jakarta during large-scale celebrations of Indonesia's 40th anniversary as an independent nation. The raising of Indonesia's red-and-white flag is part of the annual Independence Day festivities in the capital.

becoming self-sufficient in the production of rice in 1984, an accomplishment that has helped keep the enormous population relatively well-fed and healthy. The archipelago's most remote islands have been linked by Palapa communications satellites.

In international circles Indonesia has become a powerful force in the Association of Southeast Asian Nations, ASEAN, and has taken the lead in efforts to resolve political problems in the region, particularly in Cambodia. There have been occasional financial scandals, outbreaks of political unrest, and controversy over the integration of the former Portuguese colony of East Timor in 1976, government policies in Irian Jaya and the role of the military in politics. But the positive accomplishments of President Suharto's "New Order" have far outweighed the negative. For the most part, the people of Indonesia's 27 provinces are proud of the progressive accomplishments of their young nation.

Kal and I were fortunate to be in Indonesia during the celebrations of the 40th anniversary of independence. Displays of patriotic fervor animated almost every one of the villages we visited in every part of the archipelago in the days leading up to the climactic events of August 17. We spent Independence Day in Jakarta where thousands of red-and-white flags fluttered from homes, government buildings and along main thoroughfares. The air of excitement was almost palpable.

As is Indonesian custom each Independence Day morning, sirens sounded, mosque drums were beaten and church bells rang out at precisely 10:05 a.m. to mark the moment of the proclamation of independence in 1945. In moving ceremonies at the Merdeka Palace, 71 high school students, specially selected as models of their generation, marched onto the grounds dressed in pure white. The President and Vice President and their wives, cabinet ministers and military officers saluted. Diplomats from the world's most powerful nations, including the Ambassador of the Netherlands, looked on. Then one young woman from East Timor and another from North Sulawesi were presented with a replica of the original flag of the Republic. The others, who had traveled to Jakarta from each of Indonesia's 27 provinces, raised their hands in salute. As their fellow students raised the flag, they squinted into the blue sky, pride written on their beautiful faces.

Chapter Two

The People

An Account of a Journey into the Sacred Forest of the Konjo People culminates in an Audience with their hallowed Leader and serves as the Catalyst for a general Essay on the People of Indonesia, their Origins, their diverse Cultures and Religions.

Power lines hung along the narrow road leading to the village of Tambangan. But when we arrived after sunset on a cloudy October night, the only light came from the glow of kerosene lamps in the windows of some simple wooden stilt homes. Kal and I, and Daniel Rapa, our Torajan driver, were hungry, dirty and exhausted from a long, butt-bruising ride down the bumpy spine of South Sulawesi. I took some solace in a quote I had underlined that day in Joseph Conrad's *Lord Jim*:

"... do you notice how, three hundred miles beyond the end of telegraph cables and mail-boat lines, the haggard utilitarian lies of our civilization wither and die, to be replaced by pure exercises of imagination, and sometimes the deep hidden truthfulness of works of art?"

But with exhaustion setting in, art receded into the back of my thoughts. I was more concerned at that point with whether we would find food or shelter for the night or have to curl up in the van. In such circumstances, there is one certain recourse in Indonesia — head for the home of a village chief.

I know of no other country in the world where a group of strangers can barge into the home of the mayor of a town in what was tantamount to the middle of the night and not only receive a warm welcome, but get fed, get a bed and have full use of the family bathroom. At that moment I recalled the words of Cri Murthi, the head of marketing at the Indonesian Tourism Department in Jakarta who had become our good friend and ardent supporter. In a discussion a few months earlier she said, "The most basic trait of Indonesia is the sincerity of its people. It's real. There's so much beauty in this country, yet the real beauty is its people." She wasn't exaggerating.

Like the other residents of Tambangan, Headman Abdul Karim Patajai lived with his wife and children in a wooden house precariously propped above the ground on wooden pillars. The neighbors pointed it out to us. I was in a foul mood after a tiring day and stomped around the grounds aiming my flashlight at things while Kal and Daniel discussed our predicament with Abdul, but I beat a hasty retreat back to the group when my beam caught the menacing glare of a big, bushy cassowary, the family "watchbird" (some Muslims in Indonesia, like Muslims everywhere, eschew dogs), that was flexing its feathers a few feet away.

By then, our entire party was being ushered up the stairs and into the living room by the light of Abdul's pressure lantern. Young boys lugged our bags into two bedrooms that had been emptied for us. Other people peered in through the glassless windows. Steaming glasses of thick coffee were set in front of us on a polished table carved from the trunk of a tree. A lovely hardwood hutch, its shelves heavy with red-and-blue Chinese and Dutch ceramic vases, decorated one wall. Two racks that held ceramic plates hung on another. There was a glass case with a stuffed bird of paradise in a corner. I saw a big brass lamp, a small metal mosque with lights on it, two beat-up televisions and a video cassette recorder in other parts of the house, but their electrical cords all dangled uselessly.

"The government installed cables in the village two years ago, but they haven't turned on the electricity yet," Abdul told us. He said he had a generator to which he could hook up the television, but there wasn't much point because reception was

The Indonesians can be contemplative, like the solemn woman of Sumbawa (left), but more often than not they prefer a good time. Big events, and small ones, are cause for festivals like the one held in Tenggarong, East Kalimantan (preceding pages) every few years to commemorate the birth of the Kutai kingdom where jubilant participants cool off with a hosing.

bad and there were no stores in the vicinity where he could rent tapes for the video. Thus, life went on in the village of Tambangan in the district of Kajang in South Sulawesi without electrical appliances or telephones. For some of those in the district, life had changed little during the past five centuries. We were unaware just how little when we doused the oil lamps and retired.

I had a restless night. Every time someone in another room rolled over, the whole house creaked and swayed. Sleeping in a house on stilts was a lot like sleeping on a water bed. My sleepless ordeal ended soon enough. As usual in Indonesia, most of the village was up and in motion just after dawn, before the sun made it too hot to move. More thick coffee and plates of fried bananas were set out for us.

After breakfast, Abdul pulled on a black shirt, tied a black sarong around his blue jeans and wrapped his head in an indigo scarf. He was dressing out of respect for the people he was about to introduce us to, yet another of the innumerable cultures that always seems to lie just around the next bend in Indonesia. Even Kal, who was constantly subjecting himself to torturous expeditions in a neverending quest for *asli* people (those whose culture and lifestyles were not yet wholly tainted by contemporary "civilization"), had almost no knowledge of the mysterious sect we were about to meet. All we knew was that they usually wore dark clothing, spoke a language called Konjo and, thus, were called the Konjo tribe, or the people of Tanah Towa.

Abdul had arranged for a group of Konjo people from secluded *asli* villages to demonstrate their music, dance and hunting skills for us. Five men and three women met us up on a breezy hill with a pretty view. Everyone was bronzed, hale, hearty and healthy. The men wore black safari shirts and sarongs and headdresses of black or indigo blue, the women dark blouses and sarongs except for one who had tied a red ribbon in her ebony hair. Without much fanfare, two of the men began puffing out a melancholy melody on wooden flutes, "a sad song played at funerals" we were told. The women sang. The music mingled with the sound of the soft winds, creating an effect that was positively hypnotic.

The crowd of Konjo people grew during the course of the performance. The next song was more

Diversity is reflected in the faces and fashions of the people of Indonesia. Clockwise, from top left, are portraits of a happy islander of Sumbawa, a goateed Batak of North Sumatra, a veiled Muslim girl of Sumbawa, a man of Flores, a Dayak woman of Kalimantan whose earlobes have been distended by heavy earrings, and a beautiful Bugis girl of South Sulawesi.

The Konjo people of Tanah Towah in South Sulawesi are one of several pockets of people in Indonesia who have resisted change and live by ancient codes. Eschewing such contemporary inventions as radio and television, they entertain each other with their own handcrafted instruments, music and dance.

upbeat. Two men pounded on drums fashioned from animal skins. One of them hammed it up for Kal's cameras, striking humorous poses and grimacing, his arms and elbows flying, hands moving from the shoulders of his partner, then back to his drum. The rest of the people laughed and sang. Even Kal, jaded by years of living and moving among *asli* peoples, was impressed.

Later, a group of men rode up on the backs of pint-sized ponies. Two wild deer that had been tethered to stakes were released. One buck was so irritated it nearly gored one of its handlers with its horns, but the looks of concern on the faces of his friends dissolved into grins and giggles when the man got up and brushed himself off, shaken and scarred, but not seriously hurt. The rodeo-style roundup that followed was a raucous affair as men on foot ran about waving their arms trying to steer the deer toward the men on horseback, who in turn tried to snare the nimble-footed animal in a kind of lasso attached to a bamboo pole. One rider suceeded, only to be yanked off his mount head first by the angry buck. That incident elicited more laughter from the spectators.

I later learned from Darmawan Mas'ud Rahman, an archaeologist in Ujung Pandang, that there are about 10,000 Konjo in the mountains of southeast South Sulawesi, some clinging to more traditional ways of life than those we had met. They are believed to be among the earliest groups that migrated to Sulawesi. The most traditional of the people, those from the innermost villages, abstain from using almost every contemporary convention. They work their fields with wooden plows pulled by water buffalos (indeed the vast majority of Indonesian farmers still do), travel by horse or on foot, use primitive lamps and build their homes from wood and rattan without nails. Darmawan said the Konjo are respected by other Indonesians because they are believed to exercise strong magical powers. He explained that they choose to wear black "because it complements the simplicity of their lifestyle." They believe that people who flaunt colorful clothes have not found peace in their hearts. "Bright clothes and modern conveniences would create jealousies. Soon each man wants clothes more colorful and more material things than the next. The peace of the community is disturbed. Outside influences, even

electricity, would disturb the peace and simplicity at the heart of the Konjo culture," Darmawan said.

Elated by our discovery of a relatively unknown culture like that of the Konjo and by the day's activities, I slept better that night lulled like an infant by the rocking of the house. But the big event was yet to follow. Abdul had promised to guide us through the sacred forest to the innermost village of these fascinating people the next day, where we had had been promised an audience with the Ama Towa, the leader of all the Konjo people.

The Konjo people are only one of more than 300 cultures that flourish in the islands of Indonesia and, as our relatively easy visit to Tanah Towa proves, it is not necessary to mount a large-scale expedition "beyond the end of telegraph cables and mailboat lines," to find the kind of pristine cultures Conrad was describing when he wrote *Lord Jim*. Certainly some of the archipelago's people have been more exposed to contemporary influences that are overwhelmingly Western. Yet almost all have retained their own characteristics.

In the steaming swamps and rugged, wind-whipped highlands of Irian Jaya there are living archaeological laboratories of primitive man, the land of the Asmat and Dani tribes. On the island of Bali, an artistic flair that began to take shape more than a millenium ago colors a culture that has absorbed only the contemporary customs it wants and even then adapted them to its own uses in its own inimitable style. There are Dayaks in Kalimantan, once fierce head-hunters; good-natured Bataks in north Sumatra; and the spirited Ambonese in the Moluccas, whose ranks have produced many of the country's most popular entertainers. There are Javanese, Sundanese, Madurese, Acehnese, Timorese, Minangkabau, Torajans and Bugis. There are nearly 170-million people in all scattered around Indonesia. That makes it the world's fifth most populous country after China, India, the Soviet Union and the United States. There are discernible racial differences among the Indonesians. And there are almost as many languages as there are cultural groups, which makes the accomplishment of bringing the many groups together under one governing system even more remarkable.

The Indonesians call their multicultural, multira-

Elegant dance and music is a trademark of the refined people of Central Java. Young dancers of Yogyakarta's royal palace, the *kraton*, put in years of rigorous training to perform the intricate movements of the court dances that depict tales from Hindu epics, like the *Ramayana* and *Mahabarata*, and the island's own folklore.

cial philosophy *Bhinneka Tunggal Ika* — Unity through Diversity — a rallying cry branded into the nation's coat of arms. That spirit is manifested in certain concepts with threads that have been sewn into the kaleidoscopic tapestry of islands through the centuries. Even the most disparate groups, from the sophisticated Minahasans of North Sulawesi to the neolithic people of Nias and the Mentawai Islands, adhere to *gotong royong*, an inbred selfless social system of mutual assistance in which villagers help each other in most endeavors, worship and conduct traditional festivals together, all for the greater good of the community. Similarly, *musjawarah* and *mufakat*, Javanese practices of resolving personal and political differences through deliberation until agreement is reached, have spread to most islands and prevented potential conflict and confrontation between the cultures of the archipelago.

Despite the communal spirit, Indonesians pride themselves on their individualism and the different groups exhibit marked distinguishing characteristics. The Bataks, for instance, are customarily boisterous and outgoing, while the Javanese are soft-spoken and reserved. The people of the islands generally have considerable tolerance and a healthy respect for one another's mores but dramatic differences sometimes have erupted into conflict.

One minority group that traditionally has had troubled relations with some indigenous groups is the ethnic Chinese, the descendants of merchant and trading families who not only put down roots all over Asia but throughout the world. Their typically clannish approach to life and their economic success, affluence and influence have produced some resentment among other sectors of the populace, and even occasional hostile outbursts. Leaders in the Chinese and indigenous communities have been working hard to ease the problem, however. Even in the religious sphere, where many Chinese still cling to Taoist folk religions and its multitudes of gods in contradiction to Pancasila's One God rule, the Indonesians display uncommon tolerance. We were astonished when we went to ancient Chinese temples in the old city of Banten and in Semarang. There, we found thousands of Chinese from Indonesia and other countries peacefully offering incense, food and prayers to their gods during major festivals the same way Chinese everywhere do.

Indonesia's small Chinese minority has been influential for centuries, particularly in the economic sphere. Every year, thousands flock to *Gedung Batu*, a temple built around a grotto in Semarang, Central Java, to burn incense and pray (above and left). The festivities and temple honor Cheng Ho, an emissary from China who visited in 1406.

On Central Java's north coast in Semarang at an impressive shrine built over a cave in a cliffside in honor of the Ming admiral Cheng Ho who visited Java in 1406, workers were preparing for an influx of up to 100,000 worshipers at a festival in honor of Cheng Ho in his deification as Sam Po Kung. I met Indonesians of other faiths employed at the temple, including Muslims who were freshening up statues and friezes of deities with new coats of paint and installing booths and platforms for the socializing and feasting. There was even a *wayang kulit* shadow puppet stage near the parking lot where Javanese were putting on all night performances for all-comers. Antonius Reginald, a Hindu from Manado, said he had been employed as a driver for the festival. Pak Saeri, who was nonchalantly walking around the busy grounds in his sarong and in the boat-shaped *peci* cap traditionally worn by Muslims, told me he had worked as one of the keepers of the temple since 1972. "We're a free country. There are no problems here," he smiled.

Adat, the unwritten code of conduct and traditional practices underlying each of Indonesia's cultures, differs significantly among ethnic groups. The primitive Dani tribes of Irian Jaya, for instance, regard a long narrow vegetable gourd worn over the man's penis and grass skirts slung on the hips of a woman as proper attire. They raise and eat pigs, the fatter the better. The people of Aceh in contrast are strict Muslims who are repulsed by pork. Men routinely wear the *peci* cap and slacks, sarongs and batik shirts, while most women cover themselves almost completely and hide their hair under veils. The Balinese burn their dead in magnificent ritual funeral spectacles, while the Torajans of South Sulawesi bury their dead in an equally grand manner. The Bataks of the Toba highlands enjoy drinking and dancing and dine on dog, while other Sumatrans generally prefer soft drinks and conversation and lamb. The Minang-kabau are matriarchal, the Javanese patriarchal. The people of Sumba worship the spirits of their ancestors and the elements, those on the neighboring island of Sumbawa are devout adherents of Islam, and those on Flores mostly Catholic. In most of the Indonesian cultures, *adat* is a rigid code that governs virtually every major event in the life of an individual from his birth to his death.

Racially, anthropologists classify Indonesians into several groups. The Balinese, Javanese, Malays of Sumatra and Bugis and Makassarese of Sulawesi, considered deutero-Malays, tend to have small builds, copper skin, and Mongoloid features. The Dayaks of Kalimantan, Torajans, and Toalans, including the Konjo of Sulawesi, and Bataks of Sumatra, all referred to as proto-Malays, usually have lighter skin, almond eyes, and almost Caucasian features. The Austronesians in the eastern islands are generally bigger and have darker skin.

Intellectually, students in Bandung study nuclear physics and read classical Javanese literature in their leisure time while farmers in the nearby mountains cultivate *padi* with makeshift hoes and plows and spend their spare time grooming and training rams for the weekend fights. Artistically, the Balinese carve soft, sensuous patterns in wood while the Asmat of Irian Jaya chisel harsh, fierce faces and patterns on their shields, totems and war canoes. To some degree, the vast seas, wide rivers, dense jungles, jagged mountains and sweltering swamps have impeded cultural exchange.

The primordial landscapes and their pure cultures left such an impression on novelist Joseph Conrad during his travels as a merchant seaman that he used several of the islands as settings for some of his most important works. Only in these places, isolated from their own worlds, could his literary characters confront their darkest fears, deepest aspirations and, ultimately, the question of their own mortality. In fact, in the heart of Borneo, Conrad's tormented *Tuan* Jim was reborn as a symbol that represents "in his persistent youth the power, and perhaps the virtues of races that never grow old, that have emerged from the gloom."

It was a young Dutch military surgeon named Marie Eugene Francois Thomas Dubois who in 1892 first identified Indonesia as one of the world's earliest cradles of civilization. Dubois had steeped himself in the exciting works of Alfred Russell Wallace. Wallace's eight years of exploration and study of the Indonesian archipelago led him and his contemporary, Charles Darwin, to jointly announce in 1858 the theory of evolution that is based upon the survival of the fittest species.

Convinced he could find evidence that man

The innate creativity and good-natured sense of humor of the Indonesians manifests itself in many ways. For instance, the *bemo* passenger vehicles of Kupang, capital of West Timor, are a veritable art gallery of dancing John Travoltas, ravishing young film starlets and even grinning camels.

himself had evolved through the same process of natural selection in the very same islands that had inspired Wallace's theory, Dubois spent his spare time with his nose to the ground combing the islands for clues. After five years of digging, he sunk his shovel into the banks of the Trinil River just outside the courtly city of Solo in Central Java and uncovered the apelike skull, teeth and thighbone of a prehistoric creature he believed to be an ancestor of man. Dubois called his find *Pithecanthropus erectus* because it walked upright. Java Man, as Dubois' discovery became more popularly known, lived more than a half million years ago. Archaeologists later classified Java Man as *Homo erectus*, a cousin of Peking Man.

In 1936, another Dutchman, Dr. von Koenigswald excavated the remains of *Homo modjoketensis*, an even more primitive inhabitant of the Pleistocene Age who lived 250,000 years ago at Sangiran, north of Solo. Only later work in East Africa produced fossils of a more primitive man. Other digs at Ngandong, not far from Dubois' find, uncovered a fossil bed filled with thousands of bones of extinct mammals and 11 skulls. Archaeologists dubbed the fossils Solo Man, or *Homo sapiens*, one of the first ancestors of modern man. The remains of more advanced Australoid types have been excavated at Wajak. Primitive stone tools used by these creatures have been found throughout Java.

The experts believe small Negrito peoples were the first inhabitants of the archipelago. Australoids and Melanesians that migrated to the eastern islands after the Ice Age evolved into the Papuans. Scholars theorize that early neolithic cultures appeared in the Indonesian islands around 3,000 B.C. as so-called proto-Malay peoples from the south coasts of China and what today are parts of Cambodia and Vietnam migrated over land bridges and in double-hulled canoes at least as far east as the Polynesian islands. The Indonesian archipelago has been described as a kind of safety net under the Asian mainland that has snared groups spilling off the continent.

The proto-Malays erected stone megaliths still found in some parts of the archipelago, practiced a slash, burn and shift agriculture called *ladang*, growing rice, tubers like sweet potatoes and taro, and corn; raised pigs and worshiped the ghosts of their ancestors, a practice that occasionally involved

Crowding is common in Java, one of the world's most densely-populated pieces of real estate, but Indonesians are generally gregarious and easygoing. The typical lack of elbow room on the ferry that plies the straits between Surabaya and the island of Madura is such a common occurrence on public conveyances it fazes no one.

cannibalism, head-hunting and intertribal warfare. They believed the earth, plants, rivers, volcanos, animals, everything, including humans, possessed a spiritual life force or *semangat*.

Later, the deutero-Malays spread through the islands. They brought with them the technical advances of the Bronze Age including huge gongs. These gongs, called Dong-son drums after a culture in North Vietnam where they originated, have turned up in Indonesia in great numbers, particularly on the island of Alor in the Lesser Sundas chain where they are called *moko* and used as payment for a bride. This era also produced the prized *ikat* fiber-dyed textiles, terracing of mountain slopes for the irrigation of *padi* rice, sophisticated boat building and stone carving. Before Christ was born, the relatively-sophisticated peoples of the Indonesian islands already may have been trading with China.

By the time Purnawarman chiseled his inscriptions in West Java on the Prasasti Tugu stone, the modern ethnic composition of the archipelago was already taking shape. The Hindu influences evident by the fourth century A.D. and, later, Buddhist influences, increased as developing Indonesian kingdoms expanded trade and contacts with India. With Hinduism came the social caste systems that gave rise to class structures, especially in Java. The most important influence, Islam, arrived with Arab traders around the 12th century. But early cultures still exert a hold on some of the people of the islands.

Despite the migrations and foreign influences, historian Hall was quick to warn in his *History of Southeast Asia* against the "insidious tendency to overstress the part played by the imported cultures and to underrate the importance of the indigenous ones of the area" and noted that the islands "are not mere cultural appendages of India or China but have their own strongly-marked individuality."

A cursory look at the faiths of Indonesia illustrates how the different cultures have adapted religion to their own circumstances. Although more than 90 per cent of the Indonesians are said to subscribe to the tenets of Islam, making the country's Muslim population the largest in the world, most are nominal Muslims or practice a syncretic form of the religion. The visible trappings of Islam are all there: the mosques, the prayer mats, the jarring, amplified daily prayer calls. But Kal and I were surprised

to find almost everywhere an underlying current of mysticism and ancestor worship, practices discouraged by the Koran. In Ternate, one of Indonesia's first Islamic enclaves, people venerate the ancient crown of their sultans and in doing so the spirits of those rulers. We found the imam of an old mosque on Ai Island officiating at a blessing of sacred heirlooms, or *pusaka*, like war canoes and weapons.

A form of spiritualism called *kebatinan* mysticism shades the religions of Java. *Pusaka*, including kris daggers, leather *wayang kulit* shadow puppets, carved wooden puppets and masks are believed to have magical powers. Herbal potions and parts of animals like rhinoceros horn are used for various purposes, particularly to attract people of the opposite sex. Soothsayers, or *dukun*, are in great demand for consultation for any number of reasons, from picking an auspicious day to travel to determining when to hold a wedding ceremony or circumcision. Ceremonial *selamatan* are conducted that combine Islamic prayers with the eating of traditional dishes to ensure good luck for a marriage, celebrate a birth and other occasions.

Folkways also flavor Christianity in the islands where it has taken root. In the highlands northwest of Tanah Towa, for instance, most of the people of Torajaland have exchanged animism for Protestant beliefs. Yet some Protestant families, perhaps in a subconscious attempt to mollify all spirit worlds, abide by the age-old *adat* of staging long colorful funeral ceremonies for deceased relatives and friends in which they sacrifice dozens of pigs and water buffalos. Some Torajan groups inter the remains in cliffs "protected" by wooden effigies. The Catholics in Flores engage in vicious whip fights in a deliberate effort to spill blood on the ground which, in the past, was an essential offering to those spirits that control the earth's fertility and the harvests. Animal sacrifices and bloody rattan lashings are also part of Bali's distinctive blend of the Hindu religion imported from India with local spirit worship.

The spiritual spectrum of Indonesia has also fueled the creative fires of the people. Almost all of the temples of Java and Bali; the traditional wood-carving of the Bataks, the Dayaks, the Balinese, the Asmat and others; and the theatrical performances, dance and music that enliven the nation's cultures, have some basis in religion. In fact, many aspects of

The skin of a clouded leopard is the most stunning item of apparel in the wardrobe of an aristocrat from one of East Kalimantan's many tribes of Dayaks. The Dayaks once hunted human heads as well as wild animals. A colorful assortment of bird feathers and seashells rounds off his ensemble.

life in the islands, intercultural and intracultural, are related. Indonesian intellectual S. Takdir Alisjahbana wrote:

"Economics, law, government and the arts were not isolated human activities: in fact they were so closely interwoven that it is almost impossible to say where one began and another ended. Marriage, birth and death were not events which merely concerned individuals. The whole community was deeply involved, and such events were therefore inevitably closely regulated by social conventions. Furthermore, from another point of view, all human aims and actions were seen simply as parts of one grand natural process — the cosmic order. Only if pursued and performed in harmony with this higher, sacred Law, would an aim or an action come to a successful fruition."

And, notwithstanding the great differences between many of the archipelago's groups, Alisjahbana said that an equally large number of basically similar traits enable all of the cultures found in Indonesia to be reduced to a number of common denominators.

It is the common denominators that have been responsible for bringing the archipelago's people together in a single nation. The people of the islands now identify themselves as Indonesians, more often than as Javanese or Minangkabau or Minahasan. Cri Murthi described this increasingly communal spirit: "Javanese parents once told their daughters not to marry a Sumatran. Now there is no such thing. In my family, we have relatives from Sumatra, Maluku, everywhere," she said. "Now people think of themselves as Indonesians, not as Balinese or Bugis; one people with a common goal."

There are certain subjective observations about the Indonesians I feel qualified to make based on my many years in the islands. Perhaps the most obvious is the way people everywhere in Indonesia adore their children. Women proudly and unabashedly suckle their infants at their breast, whether they are chatting with the neighbors or flying in an airplane. Young girls love lugging newborn brothers or sisters who are almost as big as they are on their hip in a sling made from a sarong. Children are constantly caressed and spoiled, fondled and stroked, laughed at and loved, not only by family members, but by everyone within touching distance and that warmth is absorbed and stays with them into adulthood.

That people in Indonesia enjoy having children is obvious. Youngsters are everywhere. Some estimates put the portion of the population that's under the age of 15 at nearly 40 per cent. As much as Indonesians love their large families, they have realized that they have been overdoing it. Ambitious family planning programs have been implemented by the government. Despite religious prohibitions among the largely Muslim population, there are about 40,000 family planning clubs on Java alone where women from the villages are supplied with contraceptives and information. Family planning concepts are taught in the schools beginning at the primary grade levels. Many of the traditional village midwives who bring a substantial number of Indonesia's children into the world have been trained in family planning concepts. There are *dalang*, master puppeteers, who have worked family planning skits into their traditional performances. Even Indonesia's Agency for Atomic Energy has gotten into the act. In 1986, the agency announced that its scientists were conducting research into the use of nuclear energy in the production of condoms.

The programs have produced results. A study conducted over one five-year period showed family planning efforts apparently had succeeded in reducing fertility rates by 17 per cent in Central Java and Jakarta and by 15 per cent in East Java.

One trait of the Indonesian people that I found particularly easy to adapt to is a concept called *jam karet*. The literal translation is "rubber time." It means just that. Time is elastic, something that can be stretched when necessary. If an appointment is scheduled for 10 a.m., there is no reason to be outraged if it doesn't begin until 10:15.

A final observation is that the Indonesians have an unsurpassed capacity for inventiveness and a genius for keeping themselves entertained. Anywhere else, the sparks generated by the constant collision of races, creeds and cultures might explode in turmoil. Indonesians channel this energy into a creative milieu. Works of art that rank among the world's finest are produced in many islands. Hundreds of feature films are made annually. Amplified music

pours from loudspeakers on the streets of every city and village. On the national television network, new stars sing contemporary Indonesian numbers each night. Many never show up on stage or screen again. Indonesia is at once a gallery and a stage where everyone is an artist or a star.

Kal and I pulled on black shirts, sarongs and headdresses several days after our arrival in the land of the Tanah Towa. Etiquette called for us to wear the dark clothes of the Konjo out of respect for the Ama Towa, the revered leader of the Konjo people, who we were to meet that sunny day.

The Konjo people believe Tanah Towa to be a kind of Garden of Eden and that everyone on earth is a descendant of their people. They believe it was only natural for foreigners like ourselves to want to visit "our place of origin" and "our spiritual leader." So we packed some rice and black sarongs as gifts for the Ama Towa and drove into the countryside. We bounced over the rocky road through several villages and stopped at a pointed bamboo stake that had been driven into the ground. From that point on modern vehicles were prohibited. In fact it could be dangerous to drive further, Abdul told us without further elaboration. I began to feel apprehensive, a feeling that turned to alarm when Abdul pulled out a

rifle and slung it over his shoulder.

We walked from there down a road bordered by more wooden stilt homes. The power lines had now vanished altogether. Women and children occasionally stared at us from their windows, but we were not trailed by legions of noisy youngsters as we so often were in other parts of Indonesia. There was a strange silence. It was punctuated by the click of Abdul loading shells into his rifle. What had we gotten ourselves into, I wondered.

The Ama Towa lived in a large compound, but its rattan structures were as modest as any others. There were simply more of them. We removed our shoes and were shown up the stairs of one pavilion and sat down on woven mats that covered the wood slat floor. Abdul spoke a few words in the Konjo language with a man he identified as the group's minister of foreign affairs. He translated into Indonesian for us. The Ama Towa entered a few minutes later, almost imperceptibly. He sat on the floor at the head of the room. His beautiful little daughter climbed up on his lap and his pleasant-faced wife sat off to one side.

The Ama Towa's utterly tranquil face was his most striking feature and immediately put me at ease. There wasn't a trace of hostility. His eyes were deep black, shiny and penetrating. He had an

A Karo woman, wearing the customary attire of her clan, winnows rice for the day's meals outside her communal home in the highlands around Lake Toba in North Sumatra. Like most Indonesians, the Karo, the most traditional of the island's Batak people, have developed sophisticated agricultural methods.

unusually long nose for an Indonesian, but it complemented the delicate lines of his face. The corners of his lips, stained red from chewing betel, were upturned in a perpetual wisp of a smile. There was just the hint of a mustache. He moved deliberately, with the grace of a court dancer. Abdul told us the Ama Towa was 75 years old. I thought he looked 20 years younger. He said his wife, his third, was 27. The first two had passed away. He had two young children from his present wife and two from the others.

The Ama Towa fingered a tiny, ornate silver container, then unsheathed a small pestle. He fished a leaf and betel nut from an old mesh pouch, then used the pestle to crush the nut into the leaf in the container. Afterwards, he put a small ball of betel in his cheek. Abdul told us the Ama Towa had been the leader of the Konjo people for 30 years. Like every Ama Towa before him, he had been chosen during a long series of mysterious rituals held in the sacred forest, a place off-limits to all but the Konjo, where the trees and animals were believed to be imbued with spirits. A group of men, all knowledgeable in the customs, traditions, rites, beliefs and religion of the sect, and reputed to possess second sight and the power of telekinesis, are selected in initial tests. Then, they gather to await the arrival of a holy white buffalo from the woods. The buffalo walks directly to one of the select few. Then the animal is sacrificed. Priests cut off its head, lay it on a fire and watch to see if the smoke wafts toward the chosen man. Finally, piles of grain are poured on the ground in front of each candidate. A wild hen is expected to eat from the mound in front of the chosen man. Only after passing all the tests is a man named Ama Towa. He remains leader of the Konjo people until the day he dies.

Humbled by the knowledge that we had been received by such a hallowed man, we talked with the Ama Towa in polite tones using Abdul as our interpreter. The gentle man thanked us for our gifts and posed for Polaroid pictures. About an hour later, we felt it was time to excuse ourselves. Our imaginations exhausted by the experience, we lightly touched hands with the Ama Towa, said good-by and walked back down the road, back to the 20th century. Along the way, Abdul swung his rifle off his shoulder and sighted down the barrel at the limb of a tree. "Haven't seen a single bird today," he said.

On Indonesia's easternmost edge is the domain of the Dani, one of more than 200 linguistically and culturally-distinct groups who inhabit Irian Jaya, the rugged western half of the island of New Guinea. Despite life's hardships, a Dani man with bow and arrow wears the winning smile characteristic of Indonesians everywhere.

Chapter Three

Jakarta, Jakarta!

*The Author risks the first of many Rides into
Jakarta in a Taxi and Indonesia's awesome Capital City
unfolds in all its sprawling, chaotic Splendor; a movie
Poster inspires Him to ruminate on the Character of the
City and its hospitable Inhabitants.*

The average person approaches Jakarta apprehensively, bombarded with stories about its crowded squalor. I was no different. But my misgivings dissipated the first time I got into a rattletrap of a horn-honking President taxi and rode into the city. A blur of marvelous impressions and good feelings rushed past the smeared window. I tried to roll it down for a clearer look, but the handle, like those in many taxis at that time, had broken off. No matter.

I recall thinking I was watching a movie run at double speed of smiling people in constant motion, battered buses belching clouds of black smoke from their exhaust pipes, of middle-aged men with bulging calves maneuvering pedicabs through traffic-jammed side streets. Of an incomprehensible urban sprawl of tall and squat buildings, mazes of homes with red-slate roofs, ramshackle shophouses, tidy contemporary storefronts and makeshift food stalls. Of rivers of children in blue-and-white and red-and-white uniforms, pouring out of schoolyards onto the streets and sidewalks. It was all very foreign. Yet I felt right at home from the start.

In subsequent years of rambling around Jakarta, I recall stumbling upon a cinema where a huge handpainted poster advertised a film called *Jakarta, Jakarta*, a title obviously inspired by the Robert de Niro and Liza Minelli paean to New York City. Here, the appellation seemed even more appropriate. To take the analogy a step further, in Bahasa Indonesia the plural of a noun is formed simply by repeating it twice. In Jakarta, the pluralities of cultures, religions and lifestyles seem to bounce off one another like the particles in an atomic reactor, infusing the city with a boundless and contagious energy. It was ample inspiration for a writer.

A "big bang" kind of growth this century has seen Jakarta explode into a shapeless mass of about 650 square kilometers, two-and-a-half times the size of the entire island of Singapore. It is composed of a hodgepodge of kampungs, the basic village units which, like human cells, give the city life and identity. The kampungs reproduce themselves so rapidly that since the 1960s Greater Jakarta has swallowed most of the flat alluvial plains on the northwest shoulder of Java. Jakarta's suburbs have even begun inching up the bulge of volcanic mountains to the southeast.

Modest estimates put Jakarta's population at eight million in 1986, nearly double the 1971 census of 4.5 million. Family planning officials say a baby is born in the city almost every two minutes. That's 720 every day or 262,880 annually. Improving health standards and increasing life expectancies have reduced the city's death rate to only 75,000 each year. Thus the population of Jakarta is increasing by 187,000 annually, exclusive of the thousands who pour into the city from rural Java and the outer islands. An average of 10,000 people live in every square kilometer of the city, but that figure rises to 25,000 per square kilometer in the central city kampungs. That incredible concentration becomes even more astonishing when you look out at Jakarta from an airplane and find that virtually everyone lives in low-rise residences. Jakarta, Jakarta!

Jakarta is Indonesia's *ibukota*, literally its "mother city." Fertile, sensual, provocative, progressive, it has attracted people from all parts of the archipelago for centuries. King Purnawarman established the seat of his dominion, Taruma, nearby nearly 1,500 years ago. That makes Jakarta one of Asia's oldest capital cities. When the Portu-

Familiar symbols of Jakarta include the National Monument or Monas (left) which anchors the capital city's governmental district; and President Suharto and the First Lady whose visages watch over a Jakarta family from an Independence Day billboard on Merdeka Square (preceding pages).

The Muslim call to prayer from Jakarta's many mosques and the mists of a steamy tropical morning make the early hours an especially magic time in the sprawling capital. Although the number of skyscrapers in the city center is growing, most of Jakarta still consists of low-rise buildings and residences spread out over 650 square kilometers.

guese arrived in 1513, the excellent harbor at Sunda Kelapa, where the handsome Bugis *pinisi* schooners still dock, was a bustling entrepôt of the Sundanese kingdom of Pajajaran. The prominent Portuguese writer Tome Pirés, who visited in 1512, found it to be the finest harbor in Java.

Fearing the expanding might of the Muslim kingdom of Demak, the king of Sunda signed a friendship treaty with Portugal in 1522 in hopes of protecting his own interests. The Portuguese fortified the Kasteel Jakarta at Kelapa. Demak's Muslim leader Fatahillah scored successive victories over Sunda and its Portuguese allies in 1527, seized the port and to immortalize his triumph renamed it Jayakarta, the "Perfect Victory."

The Portuguese presence in Jakarta was brief but endures today in Tugu, an enclave engulfed by the civil service housing estates and noisome landfills of northwest Jakarta near the teeming Tanjung Priok industrial hub. There, a simple stucco church built for Portuguese settlers nestles in a cool copse of coconut palms and mango trees. It is cared for by the Quiko family, descendants of the area's earliest European families, who live next door.

Tugu is the birthplace of *keroncong* music, one of the most enduring reminders of the Portuguese presence. Traditionally played by small orchestras of string instruments that resemble ukeleles, Indonesia's modern composers and performers still invoke its Moorish moods in contemporary songs.

The Dutch attacked Jayakarta and wrested it from its Muslim prince in 1619. The archipelago has revolved around the city ever since. Holland's lingering presence is still evident, especially in old Taman Fatahillah which has been restored to resemble old Batavia. The grand city hall in the center of the square there has been standing since 1710. It served as the administrative quarters for both the VOC and the government and as a court and prison.

Jakarta has never been known as a pleasant city and by the 18th century it had deteriorated into a crowded, unsanitary cesspool of disease. Britain's Sir Thomas Stamford Raffles blamed some of the problems on the Dutch who neglected to provide proper sanitation and on buildings which he wrote "are admirably adapted to keep out the fresh air and retain that which is putrid or noxious."

Today, a bright team of civil servants at city hall has improved things. They have transformed Jakarta into as clean and comfortable a place as it has ever been. Dazzling rows of modern office towers, all glass and chrome, line the main thoroughfares of Jalan Gatot Subroto, Jalan Thamrin and Kuningan. Eight-lane expressways spiral and curve past the graceful meticulously-tended gardens, lagoons and sporting facilities of the Jakarta Hilton Hotel, at 13 hectares one of the most expansive luxury complexes in any city's central area and a magnet for the capital's mix of diplomats, entertainers and entrepreneurs.

Much of Jakarta is lush with tropical foliage. The Merdeka Square government district is a dramatic expanse of greenery encompassing almost a square kilometer of monuments and impressive structures built along both classical and modern lines. At its center is a 137-meter tall marble obelisk, the axis around which the city spins in perpetual motion. Erected by Sukarno, this National Monument is capped by a 14.5-ton bronze flame coated with 32 kilograms of pure gold. Northeast of the monument is austere, cavernous Istiqlal, one of Islam's largest mosques. To the northwest is Istana Merdeka, the neoclassical-style Freedom Palace, built in 1879, where the Dutch flag was hauled down for the last time in 1949 and the Indonesian banner raised in its place. President Sukarno lived in Istana Merdeka during his years in office. President Suharto has avoided the palace and its implications of royalty and lives in his own private residence in Menteng, a lovely old district of Dutch *de Stijl* architecture.

My most memorable moments in Jakarta were spent strolling through its kampungs, where most of the city's gregarious populace lives, incredible kingdoms ruled by chickens and children. Back alleys in Jakarta inevitably lead into an endless maze of narrow passages and tributaries where one small home blends into the next. In these immense domains, the most important things in life are families and friends. The sound of neighborly chatter floods every lane.

Given the nonstop carnival of socializing that Jakarta is, I frequently received invitations to visit the homes of people I met — waiters and waitresses, businessmen, civil servants, students, everyone — especially during the month of feasting that follows

The vast majority of Jakarta's population of more than seven million live in kampungs, veritable villages within the city that are self-contained and have an almost rural atmosphere. From the air, the red-slate roofs and narrow alleys of a typical Jakarta kampung resemble a gigantic maze that has no beginning — or end.

Vintage motor vehicles used as public transport and pushcarts used as mobile "fast food" restaurants are quintessential elements of the streets that skirt the crowded kampungs of Jakarta. As in the rural villages of Java, much of the business of everyday life in the big capital occurs outside the home and the streets of Jakarta are always lively.

the Muslim fasting month of Ramadan. The homes of these people inevitably seemed to be in some obscure kampung. But, despite vague directions, they always seemed confident that I would find my way. And I always did. It was as if word had been put out well in advance that if any neighbor within a five-kilometer radius saw a tall, white stranger wander by with a lost look on his face, they should escort him to the right place.

One such trip took me to the kampung of Pasar Baru, which I never realized was so awesome or so filled with people, even though the Reuters news agency office where I worked at the time was located on its perimeter in a crumbling building on the murky Ciliwung canal. The taxi dodged street vendors and chickens and scooted forward until the street became hopelessly narrow. It dropped me at the mouth of an alley that seemed to lead deeper into the maze. By then I did not have the slightest idea where I was or where I was going.

As I gingerly tested the path I soon felt like the Pied Piper. An expanding entourage of children fell in line behind me. They greeted me in both Indonesian and cute English, "Where are you going, meester? *Mau kemana?*" I told them I was looking for the home of Henny, a waitress who worked at a seafood restaurant where I had dined the night before. "You mean Henny who works at the seafood restaurant," said one boy in a combination of both languages. When I nodded, he took me by the hand and led me through winding alley after winding alley, past more children, chickens and homes with roofs that sagged under tangles of television antennas. The aromatic smell of *kretek*, the country's popular clove cigarette, pervaded the humid air. Fifteen minutes later, we stopped in front of a residence which differed little from the attached homes. Henny stood in the doorway waving.

In Indonesia, I was always treated like some long lost relative, no matter how new the relationship was. Henny's happy parents greeted me with handshakes and within minutes glasses of hot tea appeared on a table laden with bowls of peanuts and plates heaped with cakes. The cakes came in a variety of colorful designs; *kueh getuk* and *kueh mangkok* and *kueh dodol*, concoctions cooked up from eggs, sugar, flour, rice and tapioca. They had a sticky texture but a pleasant taste.

I snacked, conversed with what seemed like dozens of family members and maids and friends in my best broken Jakarta slang — within Jakarta alone there are localized versions of the Indonesian tongue — and snacked again. My concern about finding my way out of the kampung was alleviated when Henny and her pretty sisters provided safe-conduct to the main road. I was startled to find it just a few steps away from their home. I had entered the kampung at the wrong end — yet someone still realized where I was headed.

Of course, the kampungs have more than their share of pain and adversity. Despite impressive improvement programs, flooding is still a problem during the torrential cloudbursts of the West Java monsoon season. Crime is a problem, or so a scandal sheet called *Pos Kota* would have you believe. Its eagerly-read pages sensationally and graphically report lurid tales. Still, I always felt a prevailing sense of well-being in the kampungs in Jakarta and anywhere in Indonesia for that matter. Despite the obvious hardships of life, I rarely encountered the mean, despairing looks etched on the faces of people relegated to the slums of many cities in the West.

I not only wandered in the kampungs of Jakarta when I lived there, I joined in a daily ritual even more daunting to Western visitors. I rode public

buses to work. As the endless caravans of buses lurch toward the city center, their aisles fill to crushing. I was usually the only foreigner on the bus, but soon got used to the curious stares. Only the faintest glimmer of a smile on my part was enough to induce sparkling grins from most of the other passengers unavoidably, and unselfconsciously, pressed against me. I gained a great deal of admiration for those resilient, easygoing people on those long steambath rides. They managed to smile, despite the grind of waking at dawn each morning, fighting their way into a mobbed bus and standing for an hour or more. Everyone entered the bus fresh and impeccably, if simply, dressed, even though they would alight with a layer of sweat and grime. Yet they normally reached their offices and shops on time and ready for work.

President Suharto has consistently appointed progressive teams to the daunting task of running Jakarta City Hall. During the first half of the 1980s, 124 kilometers of arterial roads and 513 kilometers of local roads were constructed, the output of potable water was increased to reach at least half the city's residents and some 300,000 government-subsidized low-cost homes were built. In all, the government spent about U.S.$100 million on im-

SI SINGAMANGARAJA
1849–1907

H.RASUNA SAID

CHRISTINA MARTHA TIAHAHU

HASANUDDIN
1631—1670

PATTIMURA
1783—1817

IMAM BONJOL
1772 – 1864

provements to 537 new and 82 rehabilitated kampungs inhabited by nearly five million people. A total of 635 new schools were constructed.

Meanwhile, steps were taken to educate the population about the importance of hygiene and discipline. Rubbish trucks zigzag through the neighborhoods each day, announcing their arrival with a traditional tune called "*Jali-jali*" blaring from their loudspeakers. Television advertisements remind people to sweep garbage into closed containers, not into the streets or nearest canal, and to use pedestrian overpasses instead of jaywalking.

Jakarta's able young administrators are also in the process of implementing an ambitious program aimed at easing Jakarta into the 21st century. The plan envisions the evolution of a megalopolis called Jabotabek — a super city of more than 7,500 square kilometers and 25-million people that will absorb the adjoining population centers of Bogor to the south, Tangerang in the west and Bekasi in the east — hence, the all-inclusive acronym.

Despite its size, much of Jakarta's fascination emanates from inconspicuous nooks and intimate crannies that you might never stumble upon if you were not looking for them. One such enclave is tucked behind a modern shopping complex in the middle of Jalan Pramuka. A cacaphony of sounds emanates from a clutter of sheds and cages filled with birds and fowl at Pasar Burung, the bird market.

While the birds flutter, bicker, mate, mutter, cuddle, peck and nibble in their cages, their keepers bargain with potential buyers and compare their most prized specimens in the parking lot. Sometimes, they run birdcages up tall, bamboo poles. The height, like a treetop, inspires the birds into divine arias. But even the natural sounds of the birds are not enough for the music-loving Indonesians. The handlers attach painted wooden whistles to the tailfeathers of some of their pigeons. These birds are released from their earthbound confines at dusk when the hot, tropical, red-and-purple skies of Java shimmer, then melt in a waterfall of color.

I vividly recall a time I sat in a serene garden in Menteng exchanging sublime glances with a sloe-eyed young woman as the scent of jasmine floated on the breeze and the birds from the *pasar* took to the skies. I closed my eyes and listened. Their bamboo whistles hummed a celestial *keroncong* as the birds dipped and glided overhead, and I realized they were feathered proxies for the millions crowded into the kampungs below. Like those birds, the people of Jakarta possess the remarkable ability to soar above it all and sing in the heavens.

Soldiers, looking smart in their berets (top left), keep a constant vigil outside the Istana Merdeka in Central Jakarta. Across the street from the Istana, an Independence Day billboard (top right) honors the heroes and heroines who contributed to the development of the modern Republic of Indonesia.

Jakarta's Dreamland amusement park offers Indonesians diversions as modern as those of any contemporary metropolis. A windsurfer (top) sails past more traditional craft offshore; a family (bottom) munches snacks while hanging in the giant Ferris wheel high above the Fantasy World theme park; and, the urban landscape provides a dramatic backdrop for golfers (right).

Chapter Four

Krakatau's Children

*Being the Narrative of a Voyage aboard a Bugis
Schooner to the Realm of the Krakatau Volcano and the
last Domain of the Javan Rhino; the remarkable Tale
of the only living Foreigner to enter the Holy Villages
of the White Badui; and other Adventures on the
Islands of Java and Sumatra.*

Night fell quickly as it always does in Indonesia. There is no twilight near the equator. The sun sets and darkness moves in without hesitation. Thick clouds obscured the full midsummer moon. They wafted across the deck of the Bugis schooner and swirled around its solid wooden masts. I pulled on a sweater and a jacket, got a pillow and blanket from below and tried to sleep on deck.

The wind whipped itself into a light but cool gale when the captain spun the wheel and steered the *Bonita* south into the Sunda Straits. Sheets of lightning occasionally cut silhouettes of ominous, indigo-colored clouds on our port side where a sprinkling of lights flickered around Merak, a small harbor town on the west coast of Java. To starboard, Sumatra was invisible in the inky blackness.

Unable to sleep, I chatted with Budi, a sun-browned Samson of a crew member from Bali whose shoulder-length locks blew wild in the breezes, and Achmad, our diminutive middle-aged Bugis captain. Achmad squinted into the night and looked uncertain of himself. "It's dark," he said. "It's his first time through the Straits," Budi smiled. I surveyed the ship's ill-equipped bridge and a ship-to-shore radio strung with cords that did not seem to be attached to anything and decided I would rather sleep below out of sight, out of mind, out of harm's way. I swallowed my apprehensions as I had so often before. Bugis sailors have piloted their magnificent craft through the waters of the archipelago on a wind and a prayer for centuries.

I managed to fall into a fitful half-sleep. Oddly enough, I dreamed about a volcano. It began to erupt and I began to run. There was an incredible explosion to one side, then, as we turned to try to escape, another. Finally, sweating, I fell into a dark abyss — and a deep sleep.

The next thing I remember was the gray haze of morning filling the cabin. The clean smell of the salt air invigorated me. I poked my head out of the hatch. There, just beyond our bow, the ominous remnants of mighty Krakatau floated in the mist above the slate-colored seas.

By several accounts, the eruption of Krakatau volcano on August 27, 1883, was so powerful it was heard 4,000 kilometers away in Australia. It unleashed a destructive force equivalent to that of 10,000 megaton bombs, coughed up 18 cubic kilometers of rock and earth 27 kilometers into the atmosphere covering surrounding areas with a layer of debris up to 100 meters deep, kicked up monstrous tidal waves 30 meters high, pushed steamships 20 kilometers inland and killed 36,000 people. Ash and dust darkened the world's skies for months moving Alfred, Lord Tennyson to write: "For day by day, thro' many a blood-red eve …. The wrathful sunset glared …." More than two-thirds of the 23 square kilometer island vanished into an underwater crater seven kilometers in diameter. But by 1928, persistent volcanic activity had pushed a volatile young cinder cone above the sea. It has erupted with frightening frequency since then and has grown more than 200 meters tall. Indonesians call the virile young volcano Anak Krakatau, the child of Krakatau.

In a sense Java, Indonesia's most thickly-peopled and thickly-planted island, and Sumatra, the largest island entirely within the nation's boundaries, are both offspring of Krakatau and the family of fiery mountains that dominate their landscapes. Although the contours of compact Java are more severe than the softer curves and distinct highlands and low-

Fishing boats are moored in a steamy lagoon on Java's west coast in the village of Labuan (preceding pages). In the Sunda Straits west of Java, a fisherman warily watches an eruption of the volatile Anak Krakatau, literally the "child" of the mighty Krakatau volcanic catastrophe of 1883.

lands of Sumatra, both islands are on the Sunda shelf and structurally are part of the same fold of mountains. More than 110 volcanos, about 35 of them active, are packed onto Java which measures 1,060 meters long and ranges from 60 to 200 kilometers wide. Sumatra, 1,770 kilometers long and 400 kilometers at its widest point, has about 50 major cones, 30 of them active. Both Java and Sumatra lie in the collision zone of two tectonic plates, the Indian oceanic plate and the Eurasian continental plate. The cataclysmic clash of these subterranean slabs pushed Java and Sumatra above the surrounding seas during the late Miocene period 15 million years ago. That makes them young land masses in geological chronology that are still rocked by ongoing volcanic activity. Irrigated by almost constant streams of non-acidic volcanic debris rich in minerals, Java and parts of Sumatra also boast some of the world's most fertile land.

The two islands have also been linked through the ages by political and cultural exchange and assimilation. Most of their people are of deutero-Malay stock. South Sumatra's Srivijayan empire exerted control and influence over much of Java; later Central Java's Mataram and Majapahit kingdoms extended into parts of Sumatra. Javanese and Sumatrans dominate the present government. Islam is the predominant religion on both islands. The social and cultural links are strong.

Anak Krakatau was slumbering the morning I got my first close-up look at it from the deck of the Bugis schooner. Still, it looked deadly. We stopped briefly on Rakata, one of the now silent remnants of the island that had vanished during Krakatau's most famous eruption. We were amazed to find Rakata full of plant and bird life. It had all regenerated in the century since the great eruption.

We sailed on to the Ujung Kulon National Park, a bud of mangrove swamp and jungle on Java's western trunk where there was no evidence of the devastation caused by Krakatau, a testament to the fertility of the volcanic soils that have spawned so much life on Java and Sumatra. The Dutch designated Ujung Kulon a reserve in 1921 to protect declining numbers of *banteng*, or wild oxen, the Javan rhino, and the Javan tiger. Young rangers from Indonesia's Nature Conservation and Wildlife

Management Department now look after the 62,500 hectares of lowland rain forest, mangrove swamp and mountains. Although tigers are extinct, a tenacious campaign against poachers has helped revive the numbers of banteng and rhinos. There were only 25 Javan rhinos as recently as 1967. They had been ruthlessly hunted to near extinction for their small, single horn, which is prized as a valuable aphrodisiac in Asia. But a census conducted just before our 1985 visit indicated that the rhino population had rebounded to at least 60.

It was late afternoon when the *Bonita* dropped anchor near a weatherbeaten dock on tiny Peucang Island, headquarters of Ujung Kulon National Park. Two peacocks strolled on the white sand fringe of the island. A monitor lizard about a meter-and-a-half-long lumbered into the underbrush. Garishly-painted hornbills and kingfishers skipped through the treetops. A family of monkeys gathered and hungrily eyed our baggage and provisions.

We were welcomed by Arif Riva'i, the young head of the park's corps of rangers. His camp consisted of a few rambling wooden structures strung with light bulbs but dark for want of electricity. Wild deer hovered around the grounds. Arif proudly showed us the simple quarters where President Suharto stayed during his visits to the park and recent photographs of the celebrity whose domain they shared, the elusive Javan rhino. In recent years, the rhino has attracted the attention of foreign naturalists and photographers who spend months in the jungle recording and studying its habits — when they can find one. Later, as the sun set during dinner on the deck of the *Bonita*, a flock of hundreds of giant flying foxes glided over.

The next morning Budi took us to the mainland in a small motor skiff. A park ranger guided us through a promenade of towering nipah palms into the primeval wilderness of Ujung Kulon. A side path took us to a flat plain that could have passed for an African veldt. About two dozen banteng were grazing there. They continued chewing but surveyed our approach suspiciously. As Kal moved in for close-ups, I followed, making sure I was within leaping distance of trees that looked like they would get me out of the range of the bantengs' horns if necessary. But the herds nervously turned tail and vanished into the jungle almost noiselessly.

A Sundanese fisherman floats on a makeshift bamboo raft down a muddy river near Rankasbitung in West Java not far from the primordial jungles of Ujung Kulon (right). His checkered sarong serves many functions including that of a shawl.

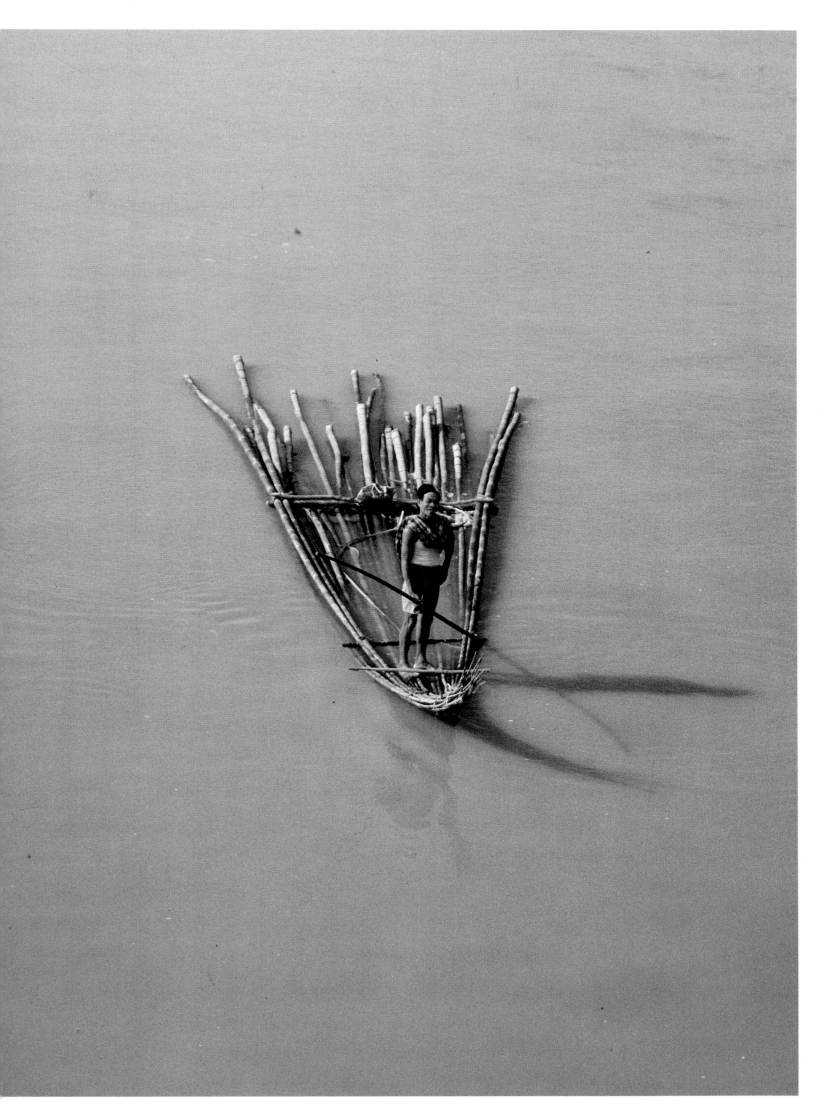

Back on the main trail, we turned into a wide, easy path cut through thickets of palms, ginger, bamboo and tall hardwoods. On the bank of a trickling creek, we saw a fresh track in the damp earth. Our guide knelt down for a closer look. "*Hari mau,*" he said and nonchalantly looked up at the branches above. A leopard! My heart stopped. I did not like the idea of walking on a trail frequented by jungle cats. Kal appeared nonplused and disappointed that neither the leopards nor any of the 80 other species of animals or 220 species of birds identified in the park were rushing out and lining up to have their pictures taken.

On the way back to the dock, our guide examined a muddy rut. "*Babirusa,*" he said, Indonesian for wild boar. By now, I was all eyes and ears. A sudden thrashing in the bush startled me. I turned in time to see a big deer dart into the trees. After several other excursions in Ujung Kulon and around Peucang Island, I learned that wildlife, no matter how big or well-equipped with claws or fangs, usually took off in the other direction when we approached. There were exceptions, of course. Wildlife photographer Dieter Plage, who stalked the Javan rhino for *National Geographic* magazine, tells of tangling with killer snakes, a cobra and a banded krait during a year in the jungle. But we were in little danger of

being pounced on by a leopard or charged by a rhino. Our ranger guides did not carry weapons, not even the handy Indonesian machete, the *parang*. A rhino never did cross our paths during our week in the park. But we sailed from Ujung Kulon content at having seen Java at its rawest.

Java's special place in the Indonesian scheme of things was beautifully delineated by C.J. Koch in his moody novel *The Year of Living Dangerously*:

"No kingdom on earth can equal this one, which is the gate of the world. Its countless islands, from the Moluccas to northern Sumatra, balanced in an arc between Asia and Australia, shield it from the storms of the Indian Ocean and the South China Sea. Active volcanos form its spine, and Visnu, its guardian god . . . protects it from all harm. Its children are more numerous, its women more beautiful, its soil more fertile: foreigners covet it. And most favored of all is Java."

Except for rare tracts like Ujung Kulon, almost every square meter of Java is populated or cultivated. More than 100 million, about two-thirds of the entire population of Indonesia, live on Java. By comparison England, which is about the same size,

Ram-fighting is one of the unusual spectator sports in Bale Ende and other mountain villages of densely-populated West Java, near the intellectual and university hub of Bandung. Two rams (above) matched by weight prepare to launch themselves into a horn-bruising collision to the cheers of onlookers. A proud owner exhibits one of his elaborately-attired prized fighters (right).

has a population of 46 million. The average density, one thousand people to every square kilometer, is misleading because the people of Java are, by nature, gregarious. They tend to congregate, not just in Jakarta, but in Surabaya in East Java, population six million; Bandung on the plateau above the convolutions of the Parahyangan area of West Java, three million; Semarang on the north central coast, at least a million; and in the Yogyakarta and Solo districts, the heart and soul of the island's cultural heartland, ten million. The networks of expressways, highways, unpaved roads, ox-cart paths and railroad tracks that link the cities to the towns, towns to the villages are almost solid with people and their shacks, *warung* (eating stalls), mansions, farms, the crumbling ruins of old and all the clutter of contemporary civilization.

The people cope with the crowding as only Indonesians can. It has brought them closer to each other in spirit as well as physically. There is a family feeling, a constant outpouring of goodwill, that spills over the mountains and plains and the *padi* in great waves of sentiment. The warmth that radiates from the people is a match for the equatorial sun. They are industrious, creative and generally happy. Yet at the same time, they are able to balance their hopes and aspirations with a keen sense of

reality. Life will go on *insya Allah* — "God-willing." The harvest will be good *insya Allah*. We will get wealthy *insya Allah*. That rhetorical Islamic refrain puts life's highs and lows in perspective as it echoes through Indonesian conversation.

Inevitably, the crowding has produced strains. Proper housing and sanitation are a problem. In an effort to alleviate overpopulation and spur on development, the government has been transplanting entire communities from Java and Bali to less-populated islands. Transmigration, as the program is called, has been a part of life in Java since the Dutch began transferring laborers to work on the rubber and palm oil plantations of Sumatra in 1905. The Indonesian government continued the policy of moving volunteers from the island after independence, but it wasn't until 1976 when the World Bank and European Economic Community development fund earmarked US$162.5 million in loans that large-scale transmigration began in earnest. Lured by free transportation, housing, kerosene, basic tools, shared livestock and plots of land, hundreds of thousands of families, roughly five million people, have pulled up roots that reach to the core of their beloved Java and transplanted themselves as pioneers in frontier developments in 20 provinces on other islands.

Long ago, European visitors began calling Java the "Garden of the East." That appellation is in no danger of becoming irrelevant. Drop a matchstick on the rich soil and it is liable to take root. In Jarkarta, mere saplings planted in the median strip along Jalan Jendral Sudirman grew into a full-fledged forest in a mere eight years. What Java lacks in the way of the natural resources of the other islands it makes up for in acres of cash crops — coffee, tea, tobacco, sugar cane and coconut.

Java's most critical crop is rice, the masses' staple and pabulum. An Indonesian without his daily rice ration is like an automobile without fuel. Powerless. Whether he takes it fried, steamed, boiled into a viscous porridge, baked into gelatinous lumps, served with a side of *satay* (meat on a skewer) or chicken (which is also prepared in an infinite number of ways) or lamb curry or grilled fish, or in sweetened colored cakes, rice is what makes him go. And Java is the nation's granary.

Java is flush with rice. The mountainsides are

stepped with it, the plains covered with it. Even in ancient times, China's Fa Hsien called Java *Yeh-p'o-t'i*, the island of "barley," his word for rice. Tidy planted rows of young shoots give the fields the texture of a hairbrush full of stiff green bristles. The necessity of this carbohydrate-rich staple comes through in the Indonesian language. It is not just rice. It is *padi* when it's in the field, *gabah* when it's unhulled and unhusked, *beras* after it's been husked and hulled, *nasi* when cooked. Irrigated plots of rice, constantly under ponds of water, are called *sawah*; dry rice fields are *ladang*.

Rice and its planting cycles are celebrated in spectacle and ritual wherever it grows in Indonesia. In order to ensure his welfare and good health, a child on Java receives seven kinds of rice cooked together with coconut milk and brown sugar in a porridge for lunch during the commemorations of his birth that occur every 35 days in babyhood. Farmers on the island of Madura, across the ship-snarled straits from Surabaya, sponsor bull races after the harvest. The best bulls are pampered, brushed, massaged and whispered magic incantations. The jockeys stand on ornate wooden harrows that are hooked behind a pair of bulls. Propelled by generous ministrations of eggs, honey and *arak*, the potent rice brandy of the islands, and blows from

the jockey's baton, the bulls thunder through the fields. The people of Madura are entertained for weeks and their fields get plowed effortlessly.

In Yogyakarta, residents build mountains of rice during a ceremony called *Tumplak Waji Garebeg Sawal* held on the grounds of Java's premier palace, the *Kraton*. They decorate the mounds with vegetables, eggs and cakes while playing the gamelan and chanting to ward off evil spirits that might infect the town. The mounds are later escorted by palace guards in a procession to the Grand Mosque where it is distributed to the people of Yogya. In Sukabumi in West Java, rice is harvested to the beat of fighting drums. The cutting of the *tumpeng*, a cone of rice, is an indispensable part of special occasions and events from weddings to the *selamatan*, a Javanese tradition that has been adopted throughout the archipelago. The Hindu goddess, Sri Dewi, is considered the patroness of rice. Many Javanese and Balinese habitually leave a spoonful of rice on their plates when finishing their meals to thank her.

From 1975 to 1980, Indonesia was the world's largest importer of rice. In 1984, the *sawah* and *ladang* of Java and the other islands yielded 25.8 million tons of rice, making the nation self-sufficient in the production of its food staple. The accomplishment was achieved through a combination of good

A farmer uses a time-tested method (above) to plow a muddy rice *padi* behind the ancient Hindu temple, the Prambanan, near Solo in Central Java; and a woman harvests tea leaves (right) on the cool, fertile slopes of dormant Tangkuban Prahu volcano.

government planning, research and development of special fertilizers and disease-resistant strains of the grain, foreign assistance programs, and backbreaking work by millions of farmers tending fields from dawn to dusk, seven days a week. Increasing production of rice on the outer islands has been responsible for the gains. But production of rice on prolific Java continues to exceed production on all the other islands of Indonesia combined.

Although the people of Java live close together out of necessity, they differentiate themselves in a number of ways. Most classify themselves as either Sundanese, Madurese or Javanese. Each of these ethnic groups has its own language and often its own way of speaking Bahasa Indonesia. The Javanese language takes various forms from low to ordinary Javanese, high, and even very high Javanese. There are the *priyayi*, blue bloods with close ties to the nobility who formed the aristocratic governing class of Java in earlier times. There are the *santri*, devout Muslims, and the *abangan*, nominal Muslims who blend ancient animist, Hindu and Buddhist influences into their beliefs. There are those who listen to new voices like that of Rhoma Irama, Indonesia's answer to Elvis Presley. Rhoma has fused amplified instruments and Islamic messages into Indonesia's *dangdut* musical form, giving it an electric, hip-grinding beat, a kind of Western technobop with an Eastern message. And there are those playing the same old songs that have echoed in Java for thousands of years, notably the Badui, a mysterious, reticent sect of about 10,000 who live in the mountains of West Java.

Believed to be the direct descendants of the ancient kings of Sunda, the strictest Badui obey a rigid set of taboos that forbids the use of electricity, chairs, beds, tables, flashlights, liquor, shoes, sandals, drinking glasses, motor vehicles and virtually every other byproduct of progress. They are loyal to three holy men known as *Pu'un* and live in villages deep in the mountains of West Java that are off limits to all but fellow Indonesians. The 40 families of the three "inner" villages dress exclusively in white clothes and turbans and safeguard the secrets of the old religion of ancestor worship. The inner sanctuaries are protected by a ring of villages of "outer" Badui who, like the Konjo of Sulawesi,

dress in dark clothes of black and indigo blue. Outer Badui are more flexible in their approach to the taboo system and act as intermediaries between the inner White Badui and the outside world.

Intriguing stories surround the fabled temple mount of the Badui, Arca Domas. The name is Sanskrit for 800 and is thought to be a reference to the number of people who fled into the mountains 400 years ago and founded the sect. Only Badui are permitted to see Arca Domas. Only they know its precise location. Some say Arca Domas is a complex near the source of the Ciujung River with a shrine of 13 terraces at its core, the island home of Batara Tunggal, the "one-god." When the White Badui die, they believe their souls travel to the core of Arca Domas to be reunited with the universal soul of Batara Tunggal. The shrine is said to be embellished with statues of horses, goats and water buffalos and the southern portal of Arca Domas is reputed to be guarded by a live, venomous scorpion. It is through this southern gate that Batara Tunggal enters the shrine during one of the rice harvest festivals held each year. He comes for his "bride," a female fertility figure fashioned from rice dough which is carried to Arca Domas by the Badui in a procession together with an egg and a live tarantula.

Perhaps the only foreigner to ever enter the inner

villages of the Badui this century is Ian Morgan, a trekking enthusiast and longtime resident of Indonesia who is managing director of a Jakarta property company. Kal and I chatted with Morgan during a respite at the rustic Hotel Krakatau on Carita Beach, a popular starting point for visits to Badui country and Anak Krakatau. Although as respectful of the privacy of the Badui as the Javanese, Morgan said he stumbled into their realm by accident while hiking in the jungles of southwest Java in 1976.

"I had been walking for about a day with my guides just on the other side of the Cidikit gold mines when we came upon this line of wild-looking windmills, all fashioned from bamboo, all screaming at us in the wind. It would be quite frightening if you strayed into that area at night. I guess the windmills are designed to scare away evil spirits.

"We continued over a ridge of bamboo. I figured my guides, who were from the local villages, knew where we were going, but I guess none of us realized how near we were to Cibeo, the holiest of the inner villages of the Badui. I didn't realize it until we came across a field where a group of White Badui were picking durians, their main export commodity. Then we came to a village just beyond a clearing which had these amazing sloped buildings for storing grain. It's probably a good thing we entered the village when most of the people were out in the fields. I'd read all the books about how they poison you if you disturb the sanctity of their villages. But we met an old man who was very courteous. He had a high, squeaky voice, a small build and was barrel-chested like a lot of the others we met. Apparently a lot of the Badui have rickets. There's a lack of Vitamin A in their diets.

"The village itself was very pretty. I soon realized we were in Cibeo. The carving on the houses was impressive. We didn't spend more than an hour there. The old guy wouldn't let us look around. But we were permitted to spend the night in a little village outside Cibeo. We were a bit nervous about that after all the stories we'd heard, but the people served us a nice meal. They asked us for medicine. Although we'd been told they don't accept any modern manufactured items, they did accept a gift of a metal hunting knife from me. From there I picked up some Badui guides.

Trays of tobacco, cultivated by the Gudang Garam *kretek* cigarette company, are dried
in a soccer field in the Central Java village of Kledung after the May harvest. In the
distance, clouds dust the 3,370-meter Mt. Sumbing. The effluent from Sumbing and other
volcanos is not acidic so it has made Java incredibly fertile.

The guides turned us over to the Black Badui in the outer villages. On the way out we were told the old man we'd met in Cibeo was one of the *Pu'un*. That was when I understood why all my Indonesian guides had walked to the other side of the road when he came out of the woods. It's very unusual to meet a *Pu'un*. The whole trip took about four days. Later, I learned that I'd been the first foreigner to get into the inner villages since a Dutchman named Koorders did it in the 19th century. And return to tell about it. Something strange did happen, though. I'd managed to take some photographs in the Badui villages. They really don't like that at all. I had the film processed when I got back to Jakarta. It was blank. There wasn't anything on it."

Kal and I spent a night with the black Badui in their outermost village, Kaduketug. The trip there was a hemorrhoid-inducing ride south from Rankasbitung through Leuwidamar where we checked in with the *polisi*, as we always did, up and down a mountain road studded with stones and boulders over which we bounced to the beat of electrified Middle Eastern pop which incessantly blasted from the cassette deck of our driver, an Indonesian of Arabic parentage named Zet. I took to calling him "Jet" in deference to his driving habits.

Jet's Colt van balked at one slippery slope and a group of young men helped us haul it up the hill with a rope. We walked from there through a typical Java village up a path into the forest, through a makeshift wooden gateway that said "Welcome to the Land of Badui" in English, and under a bamboo tube fixed between two cliffs, a bridge in a system of tubes used to catch water in a trough for washing and drinking. The simple, *atap*-roofed wooden dwellings of Kaduketug were set close together in a sunny clearing of banana palms. A few barebreasted women grabbed their children and dashed into their homes when we arrived, then gawked at us from their dark doorways. A few others continued weaving on wooden looms on their porches without giving us a second glance.

We were promptly ushered into the home of the village chief, the *Jaro*, Nakiwin. He accepted our gifts of bags of *beras* (raw rice), *kretek* cigarettes and canned food without remark or emotion. The *Jaro* and his family had no objections to having their

***Krupuk* biscuits made from prawn, rice, vegetable or crab paste** are a favorite
Indonesian snack. Before frying, the cakes of *krupuk* are dried in the sun in villages like
Kediri on the north central coast of Java covering the fields, roadsides, even the roofs of
homes with a riot of color. When fried in oil, the cakes expand into tasty crackers.

The mysterious Badui sect have isolated themselves from the 20th century in remote West Java mountain villages where daily life has changed little in five centuries. The portraits above depict a Badui mother and child (left) and Jaro Nakiwin, headman of Kaduketug (right). Below, a Badui builds with bamboo.

A curious Badui child peeks from the door of her home (top left), a group of Badui men and women return on foot from a visit to a neighboring village (top right), and a woman weaves fabric at her loom (bottom) on the porch of her bamboo and rattan home.

Every Sunday at the Kraton, the historic palace of Yogyakarta's long line of sultans, aspiring young men and women twist their supple bodies into the difficult movements of Javanese court dances. The weekly rehearsals occur under the discerning eye of past dance masters. Here an instructor adjusts a student's headpiece.

photographs taken. When Kal pulled out his Polaroid and began passing out instant pictures, the entire village was soon lining up for portraits.

I spent most of my time sitting inside on the palm mat floor talking to *Jaro* Nakiwin with one of our guides translating his old Sunda language into Bahasa Indonesia for me. The *Jaro* had a finely-chiseled face with high cheekbones. His expression clearly intimated that here he was the boss. Other than an exquisitely-cast gamelan set in one corner of the room and some civil service calendars, photographs and the customary portraits of Indonesia's president and vice-president on the wall, the room was devoid of furnishings. A batik sarong tied to a roof beam was used as a bouncing cradle for a baby. A dark inner room had a smouldering wood-fire hearth for heating and cooking. Simple utensils and brass pots dangled from hooks on the wall.

As is so customary when visiting in Indonesia, our host pulled out albums of family photographs for us to admire. One contained a newspaper clipping that showed the *Jaro* meeting with President Suharto in his government office in Jakarta. Although his superiors, the *Pu'un*, had been known to walk all the way to Jakarta, the *Jaro* said the President sent a car for him and he agreed to ride in it. He said the President asked about living conditions in the Badui villages and whether the people were healthy and had enough to eat. I asked the *Jaro* how he dressed for his meeting with the president. He looked at his bare feet, black sarong and shirt and touched his blue turban. "Just like this," he said. It was the only time a grin cracked the *Jaro*'s molded emotionless countenance during our visit.

It started to rain heavily late that afternoon. The Badui put on floppy, wide-brimmed palm hats that extended over their shoulders and darted between the houses. There were eight visitors in all and we crowded into the *Jaro*'s home, five in our party and three Indonesian medical students from Bandung who were studying the health of the Badui, especially the skin diseases that plagued many of the children, and were administering medicines. Medicine was one form of magic from the modern world both the White and Black Badui eagerly accepted.

As the intensity of the rain increased, we all shared a simple meal prepared by the *Jaro*'s wife from the provisions we had brought; some rice,

canned fish, hot chilly peppers and cups of coffee thick with grounds. That night, mats and pillows stored on bamboo slats above the room were laid out for us. Jet went out to his van and returned in a few minutes elegantly dressed in pressed cotton pajamas. We all slept in a huddle, toe-to-head, elbow-to-knee, lullabyed to sleep by the splash of the raindrops and the soothing chiming melodies played on the gamelan for honored guests.

Central Java is the cultural and creative cradle of Indonesia. Its refined, sensitive people began manufacturing beauty long before the cathedrals of Europe were erected. In Yogyakarta and Solo, in rooms open to the sunlight behind airconditioned showrooms, women hunch over bolts of cloth laboriously penciling patterns with *canting* pipes of hot wax making classical and contemporary styles in batik, the popular textile of the islands used in everything from tablecloths to elaborate wedding ensembles. Thousands of other women work in factories in Kudus and Kediri handrolling millions of *kretek*, the fragrant clove cigarettes that some serious smokers consider an artistic achievement.

Other art worlds — painting, carving, sculpture — are dominated by men. In Kota Gede, dozens of them, young apprentices and old experts, squint in smoky rooms where they pound and polish plates, pots and jewelry made from silver. A few aging men still forge the blades of the powerful symbol of the gender, the kris dagger, in some villages. On the north coast east of Semarang, craftsmen specialize in chiseling entire reliefs of warriors, chimerical creatures, princesses and landscapes on wooden furniture. Some artists, like the abstract painter Affandi, are internationally recognized. His brush strokes command such high prices that he can afford to work out of an abstract adobe studio in Yogyakarta.

The patterned *padi* and terraced mountainsides of Central Java around Yogyakarta and Solo are works of art in themselves. The young rice stalks sway in the balmy breezes as if to the rhythms of gamelan orchestras, ancient instruments that look like brass pots and pans which when banged with hammers produce music that Dutch scholar Jaap Kunst perceptively compared to "moonlight and flowing water." The Hindu literary epics, the *Ramayana* and *Mahabarata*, provide fodder for raucous shadow puppet performances that fill entire evenings with the mystery of the ages, the click-clack of *wayang golek* — wooden puppets — and classical dance. Precision movements are painstakingly passed on to new generations of dancers in the stately pavilions of the *kraton*, or palace, each week. I spent several

evenings under the full moon watching dancers undulate to the gamelan music as they enacted the timeless tales of the *Ramayana* on a stage in the forecourt of the ancient Pramabanan temple. The grand performances breath new life into the regal old stones.

The Javanese are rarely thought of as great architects, yet as Sir Thomas Stamford Raffles noted after uncovering the ruins of Borobudur in 1814: "The interior of Java contains temples that, as works of labor and art, dwarf to nothing all our wonder and admiration at the pyramids of Egypt." Even when cluttered with construction cranes, with hundreds of its *stupas* and Buddhas and stone reliefs strewn about at its base, as it was during its reconstruction, the inconceivable sight of Borobudur never failed to move me. Its charcoal-colored granite terraces, unearthly in their bearing and power, stand out against the virescent peaks, a cosmic mountain rising in the lee of smoking, dangerous Mt. Merapi and in the shadow of Mt. Tidar, the nail in the island's navel that holds Java in the center of the sea.

Built by the Sailendra kings during the eighth and ninth centuries, 200 years before Notre Dame and 300 years before Angkor Wat, Borobudur embodies the essential precepts of Buddhism. It endures as a magnet for the faith, attracting thousands of worshipers and shaven-headed, saffron-robed monks from around the world during the Waisak celebrations held there each May. Originally, Borobudur consisted of ten levels that represented the stages in the Buddha's transcendence from earthly frivolities and limitations. The story is documented in galleries of stone reliefs of the Buddha's life. His spiritual escape from earthly bonds is symbolized by the lack of all ornamentation starting at the fifth level. The circular terraces above are punctuated with bell-shaped latticed *stupas* that have statues of the Buddha inside. Finally, the Buddha's rise to the formless, abstract state of heavenly perfection is implicit in the eight-meter high main *stupa* at the sanctuary's pinnacle.

Borobudur, its treasures plundered by greedy foreign "collectors," deteriorated after Raffles revealed it to the world. It was not until the 1970s that concerned member nations of UNESCO stepped in and offered to help restore Borobudur. Eight years of work and about U.S.$60 million from UNESCO nations ended when President Suharto officially dedicated the rejuvenated monument in February, 1983.

The restoration is impressive. The Indonesians, with their inimitable sense of aesthetics, have laid a long, wide, landscaped carpet of flowers to the temple. The initial impact of Borobudur shimmering in the layers of moist tropical heat at the end of that passage is stunning. During the protracted walk

The awesome Borobudur, the world's largest Buddhist stupa, epitomizes the classic artistic traditions of Central Java. Built by more than 50,000 craftsmen over a period of 78 years in the eighth and ninth centuries, the Borobudur was recently restored by a large corps of skilled Indonesian craftsmen.

to the foot of the temple, Borobudur grows until it fills the horizon. By the time you mount its steep stairs and climb into the maze of galleries, the senses are overwhelmed by its size and symmetry.

The first time I visited Central Java was in the summer of 1978 with a study group from the University of Hawaii. We stayed in Yogyakarta in the clean, unpretentious Srivijaya Guest House of the genial family of Atmohartono. It was in a narrow lane that, like so many roads in Indonesia, had a mix of humble homes with makeshift communal badminton courts and Ping-Pong tables of the low income groups adjoining the rambling, walled-in mansions of those who were much better off. Each morning, dozens of eager men lined up at the entrance to the guest house perched on their brightly-painted *becak*, three-wheeled pedicabs in which passengers ride up front, lobbying for paying customers.

On my first of many, many *becak* rides in Indonesia, fate matched me with an affable driver named Sarjono who was about my own age. Sarjono spoke a smattering of English and, like most Indonesians, exuded optimism and charm in spite of the fact that his was a grueling occupation. He pedaled about a dozen people a day more than 30 kilometers through the rutted and potholed roads, up and down inclines through suffocating heat and sudden explosions of rain. Sarjono introduced me to the enchanting back alleys of Yogyakarta, to the brash batik artists of Taman Sari, the Water Castle, to the bustling central market and funky tourist cafes and souvenir shops of Marlioboro Street. As if by some extraordinary sense of perception, he seemed to pedal up whenever I was in need of a lift.

As the years went by, I got to know Sarjono well on subsequent trips to Yogya and I featured him in a story about the life a *becak* driver, the most obvious of Indonesia's multitude of unskilled laborers. Sarjono managed to care for his wife and two children on earnings amounting to the equivalent of about U.S.$3.20 a day and lived in a rattan-walled hut shared with another family. He had high hopes of one day graduating from driving a *becak* to driving an automobile, so he could make more money and put his children through high school so that they would be able to get better jobs. The story and a photograph of Sarjono driving his *becak* down a gravel road in Yogyakarta with an ebullient expression on his face was prominently featured in the *Washington Post* and was subsquently picked up by dozens of newspapers around the world.

Not long afterwards, I left Indonesia. I did not return to Yogyakarta until five years later when Kal and I took an overnight train there from Jakarta. Sarjono had not crossed my mind for years, not even when we checked into the old Srivijaya Guest House. It had been swamped by fancier guest houses and cafes catering to tourists but little else had changed on the narrow lane. The contingents of *becak* boys still gravitated there looking for fares.

From that base, Kal and I decided to rent a car to cover Central Java. Pak Atmohartono (Pak is short for *bapak*, father in Indonesian, and the common honorific for men) pointed us down the road toward a neighbor's house. We sat down with an agent and a driver in the dimly-lit hall filled with antiques and began negotiating a price. By then, I already sensed a familiar presence, but I wasn't quite sure why. I nonchalantly glanced at the man who was to be the driver of our car. Then I looked at him again harder. He returned the glare, a grin curling from the lips of his affable face.

Sarjono! Five years had passed, yet the mystic forces that pulse through Central Java had thrown me and Sarjono together yet again. We clenched hands and slapped each other on the back. Then Sarjono reached in his pocket and pulled out a tattered yellow newspaper cutting. It was the story I had written about him clipped by a visiting tourist who had searched out Sarjono to be his *becak* driver.

Sarjono and I talked as Kal continued negotiations. As it turned out, he had succeeded in stepping up in the world, from a barefoot *becak* boy into the shoes of an automobile driver. Not only that. He said he had begun an association of *becak* drivers that helped negotiate fair rental rates with the owners of the vehicles. His children had grown up and he was putting them both through high school. Now that he drove motor vehicles, Sarjono said his next goal was to purchase his own car for hire.

Kal finally arrived upon a satisfactory price with the owner. A few minutes later an old Dodge rumbled up to the front gate. Sarjono, well-dressed and grinning, was at the wheel. As I closed my eyes in the back seat the years fell away. They sometimes do in Indonesia.

Descended from sultans, aristocrats and artists, the people of Central Java wear their illustrious heritage proudly (right). Because they constitute the majority of the island's 100 million people, the Javanese continue to wield a powerful influence over the entire Indonesian archipelago as they have for centuries.

Most of Sumatra is a stronghold of conventional Islam, particularly the northernmost province of Aceh. The *Masjid Raya*, the Grand Mosque (above), graces the provincial capital of Banda Aceh. Early this century its classic lines were fashioned from wood without the use of a single nail. Like traditional dwellings of Aceh, it is held together with a sophisticated system of dowel joints and wedges.

On the map, Sumatra resembles a fish that stretches 1,600 kilometers in the Indian Ocean from snout to tail, from Java almost to India's Nicobar Islands, and is bisected about midway by the equator. A volcanic spine, the Bukit Barisan or, appropriately, "parade of mountains," runs almost the length of the island and is crisscrossed by raging rivers and speckled with crater lakes.

Although Sumatra is three-and-a-half times the size of Java, it has less than a third of its population. Cultural groups are sprinkled in nooks and crannies that, in contrast to Java's, are relatively isolated from one another by the craggy surface; a niche of fundamentalist Islam in Aceh on the tailfin; a touch of Christianity around Lake Toba above the scurfy dorsal; a mixture of Islam and ancestral *adat* around Bukittinggi and Padang on its southwestern flanks; scattered areas of prehistoric animism on the islets suspended like pilot fish on its underbelly.

If flora and fauna are found on an island in the western part of the archipelago, Sumatra is likely to have it too, and much more; tigers, orangutans, foxes, elephants, rhinoceros, crocodiles; 60 meter tall ketapang (*terminalia catappa*), waringin, banyan, rubber, palmetto, *alang-alang* sedgegrass. A Hungarian who established a tobacco plantation in Sumatra about 1902, Ladislao Székely, found the island so exotic he wrote, "If there had been seven-footed calves or nine-headed cows in this region, I should not have been astonished."

Sumatra is so large and diverse, the government has subdivided it into eight administrative provinces. In terms of resources, it is Indonesia's richest island. Oil has been pumped from its innards for more than a century. The Minas field that Riau province floats atop, has produced more petroleum than any other in Southeast Asia since Dutch geologists began drilling there in the 1880s, fueling the economy of Indonesia and other parts of the world. Natural gas has been tapped at the large Arun field in Aceh Province and is liquified at a plant in Lhokseumawe. Tin is mined and smelted in the Bangka Islands. Sumatra is also an agricultural wonderland. Rubber, palm oil and delicious Arabica and Robusta coffee beans are cultivated on immense plantations in the hills and vast rubber and palm oil tracts blanket the southeastern flatlands, an area that has been called "a vast commercial garden."

More than 3,000 faithful Muslims bowed down as Kal watched, praying in unison. It was a Friday evening, Islam's Sunday, during the fasting month of Ramadan. The utter submission to Allah and faith in His religion was almost tangible.

Kal had obtained permission that special night to photograph at the resplendent Grand Mosque in Banda Aceh, the capital of Indonesia's most devoutly Islamic province. The Dutch built the mosque as a goodwill gesture, after burning down another when they invaded the recalcitrant realm at the northern tip of Sumatra in 1873. Sukarno in turn added the cupolas and minarets in 1956 also as a goodwill gesture, after the Indonesian army invaded to put down rebels who wanted to make Aceh an independent Islamic Republic. Powerful *ulamas*, Muslim leaders, agreed to a ceasefire in 1957 on the condition that Aceh be designated a special province with a high degree of control over its internal affairs. Aceh has had a tough reputation as an almost fanatical bastion of Islam ever since.

That reputation wasn't lost on Kal, a lapsed Catholic, who approached the packed mosque nervously. Even the reassurances of the imam, the prayer leader, failed to lessen his apprehension especially when the swarthy holy man led him to the *mimbar*, the pulpit at the front of the congregation, and told him he could take his photographs from there. Thousands of men, some wearing the white skullcaps that identified them as *haji*, men who had made the pilgrimage to the holy K'aabah in Mecca, knelt on prayer rugs up front. Some gave Kal and his cameras a suspicious look. Behind them, in a separate area as is Islamic custom, rows of women swathed in white robes and veils faced Mecca. But prayer soon absorbed all the worshipers and Kal snapped away without incident. After he finished, he stayed behind mesmerized by the spectacle of thousands prostrating themselves then kneeling upright, palms cupped to the heavens in prayer, in impossibly perfect unison. Kal came away from the mosque convinced that the people of Aceh were more tolerant and amicable than they have been portrayed in the media.

Still, the trip from Aceh to other parts of Sumatra can be as jarring as the ride from Jakarta to the Badui villages. In the neighboring province, the Batak people practiced cannibalism into the present century. Bataks punished traitors, spies, deserters, their enemies and commoners who committed adultery with one of the raja's wives, by eating them — sometimes while they were still alive. One German missionary who witnessed the practice wrote that a victim was bound to a stake in front of

the village people and excoriated for his evil deeds while "the people water at the mouth and feel an irresistible impulse to have a piece of the criminal in their stomachs, as they will then rest assured that he will do them no further harm." During his travels in Sumatra in the 19th century, Raffles observed that the diner's preference was for the palms of the hands and feets, raw or grilled, and lightly flavored with lime, salt and pepper and a side order of rice.

The original Bataks worshiped their ancestors in extraordinary rituals and carried long magic wands, but many were converted to Christianity by German missionaries during the 19th century. A minority of Muslim Bataks live to the south around Mandailing. The most traditional Bataks, the Karo, live to the north around Lingga. A few of the Karo still cling to some animist traditions. For instance, when a youth in the community dies, special care is taken to insure its spirit will not become a bother out of sexual frustration. If the deceased is a young man, the penis of the corpse is encased in warm bamboo. If it is a girl, a banana is inserted in the vagina.

About a million-and-a-half Bataks live in Sumatra. Most are concentrated in the highlands around Lake Toba, a body of water cradled in a volcanic depression 800 meters above sea level, the most splendid of the deep crater lakes in the Bukit Barisan. Toba is Indonesia's largest lake and one of its most popular vacation resorts for water sports and fishing. It covers 1,707 square kilometers. Almost a quarter of that is filled by Samosir Island which itself is larger than all of Singapore, the independent island republic to the southeast. Steep velvety green slopes, decorated with the characteristic saddle-roofed houses and rice barns of the Batak, circle Toba's perimeter and plunge into the water to depths of up to 450 meters.

A Batak legend tells of the creation of the lake. A farmer who lived in the area was fishing in his favorite stream when something big caught in his net. What he thought was a fish turned out to be a beautiful young woman named Saniang. The farmer promptly fell in love and Saniang agreed to marry him on the condition that he never reveal her unusual origins.

Saniang gave birth to a son after the wedding. One evening when the boy had grown into a teenager, he came home to find his father's dinner laid out on a table. On impulse, the hungry young man devoured the meal. The father, who returned from the fields famished, went into a rage when he found his table empty. "You uneducated son of a fish," he shouted so loud the whole village could hear. Furious that her husband had exposed her secret, Saniang's supernatural anger caused a volca-

Inside the Grand Mosque in Banda Aceh, the faithful pray in the same manner as Muslims everywhere. Modestly veiled women (left) are segregated behind the greater numbers of men who kneel on prayer mats in the front of the mosque (right).

no near the village to bubble and explode. Then a violent thunderstorm poured rain for weeks. When nature's fury subsided, the village was gone. All that was left in its place was Lake Toba.

Another nugget of folklore is associated with the Minangkabau, the major cultural group of West Sumatra, a land of rolling thunder, gentle mountains, waterfalls, rivers and lakes, arguably Indonesia's loveliest scenery. During the golden era of Majapahit, Javanese armies conquered Palembang in South Sumatra and pushed out to the west which at the time had its capital at Pagarruyung. The Javanese sent a messenger to Pagarruyung demanding that it surrender. In return, the West Sumatrans sent an adviser with a letter written on a palm leaf challenging the Javanese to a duel of *kerbau*, or buffalo, in order to avoid human bloodshed. Confident that the mighty *kerbau* of Java could defeat those of Pagarruyung, the Javanese commander agreed to the contest and promised that he and his armies would retreat if his animal was defeated.

Preparations were made for a great festival in the capital. One hundred of the Javanese officers were invited to the Pagarruyung square. On the day of the competition, they astonished the villagers with their combatant, a strong buffalo with horns a meter long sheathed in gold. The Sumatrans, in contrast, led a thin, pathetic-looking calf into the arena eliciting laughter and insults from spectators on both sides. But the catcalls soon turned to surprised approval. When the calf saw the big *kerbau*, it thrust its head into the buffalo's belly to suckle. But the buffalo backed away as if in pain. Each time the calf tried to suckle, the buffalo ran off with the weaker animal in hot pursuit to cheers from both sides. Finally, the *kerbau* fell dead, blood streaming from its stomach, and the Sumatrans revealed their clever ploy. They had starved the young calf for several weeks, then, before sending it in against the *kerbau*, fixed a spike-studded steel plate in its mouth. When the calf tried to suckle, the barbed plate eventually disemboweled the buffalo. The Javanese acknowledged their defeat and retreated as promised. West Sumatra has been called *minang kabau*, meaning "victorious buffalo," ever since.

The buffalo is an integral element in the architecture and dress of the region as well as in its folklore. The magnificent communal houses and council halls of the Minangkabau are topped by roofs that curve into points like horns. The number of roofs traditionally indicated the size of its owner's family. Fashioned from stiff palm fiber, some roofs have as many as a dozen gables. Walls are carved and painted with colorful vertical bands, spirals and scroll motifs. Many of the Minangkabau's mosques, like ancient mosques in parts of Java and the Moluccas, hark back to the influence of Hindu Srivijaya. The traditional dress of Minangkabau women, like the architecture, is a visual feast. They wear pointed headdresses that reflect the buffalo horn motif of the region's rooftops. The rich fabric in these ceremonial outfits is heavily embroidered with gold and silver threads.

The most unusual aspect of Minangkabau society, given the male orientation of Islam and most of Indonesia's cultures, is that women head the families. Minangkabau women maintain hereditary rights to the land, rice fields and houses. They are heiresses to all family possessions. Families are called *saparuik*, meaning "from one womb," and descendants are identified through the female line. In this matriarchal system, it has been customary for the girl's family to choose a mate for their daughter rather than the other way around. Consequently, the women bear the brunt of the wedding expenses and put up the dowry which, in the early stages of marriage, is little more than a payment for the husband's stud services. The husband spends a night with the woman at her household, then leaves and usually has to be fetched back to the marital bed by his wife's family for the next few nights.

Since men have no stake in the family home, they traditionally left the family and sometimes the island to seek their fortune, sleeping in mosques and eating in restaurants, one of the wry explanations offered by tour guides for the large number of restaurants throughout the archipelago that serve Padang cuisine. (The cuisine consists of a dozen plates heaped with meats and vegetables marinated in caustic, tongue-singeing spices and takes its name from the tidy capital city of West Sumatra.) The nomadic lifestyle of Minangkabau men is institutionalized and called *merantu*. It has taught them to live by their wits and has turned them into shrewd merchants as well as restaurateurs. A man who

The mythical influence of the water buffalo extends even to the traditional attire of West Sumatra's people. The headdress of this Minangkabau woman resembles buffalo horns. The artistic Minangkabau men carve lovely swirling patterns into the window sills and other woodwork of their homes.

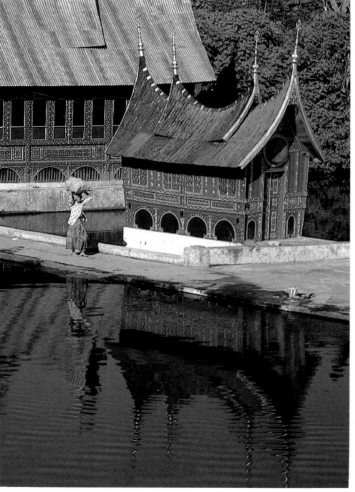

makes his fortune is expected to return to his wife and sisters. While women run the all-encompassing households, local government is still the purview of males and each family chooses a man to represent them in the village councils. Even in matriarchal Minangkabau women stay out of politics.

The only time I got anywhere near Palembang while traveling in Indonesia was on a stopover at its modest airport in a light Cessna. It had been chartered by Continental Oil Company (Conoco) to fly some of its executives to Tanjung Pinang to catch a connecting Puma chopper to offshore oil and gas operations near the Anambas Islands where I was headed to visit the refugee camps of Vietnamese boat people. The small plane touched down smoothly, but its nose stayed above the pavement until we came dangerously close to the end of the runway. Apparently the pilot had let his flight engineer "practice" landing and had resumed control and gotten the nose down only inches from disaster.

Nonetheless, we picked up another Conoco employee and got back in the plane. My thoughts turned to Garuda, the mythical heroic bird who perishes trying to rescue a princess from the clutches of an evil demon and who has been adopted as the patron of Indonesia's national airline. Then I cast my fate to the wind. The pilot taxied to the runway and gunned the engine. Just as he was to take off, he slammed on the brakes. A dog had darted on to the runway. The pilot turned the plane around and headed back down the airstrip for another try. This time we made it back into the skies, but I kept my eyes on my folded hands and never looked back.

Because of natural resources like oil and tin, the Riau Archipelago, where we landed without further incident and happily transited to the Puma on Bintan Island, has developed into an adjunct of the industrialized world, a way station for tankers and aircraft. The Riau Islands are used like stepping stones to the Malay Peninsula by fishermen and sailors. Batam, clearly visible from the financial district's skyscrapers on the ultramodern independent island nation of Singapore, is being developed by the Indonesian government into a bonded zone and industrial estate and a getaway resort for people from both countries. Further east, Bangka and Belitung are dusty centers for tin mining.

Idyllic scenes in West Sumatra's countryside. Men relax under the Arabic archways of a mosque (top left) and a scaled down version of a Minangkabau dwelling serves as a rice barn (bottom left); a full-sized version of the grand communal homes of the Minangkabau graces a *padi* near Padang (above) and a mosque enhances a valley in the Bukittinggi highlands (bottom).

Conversely, the major islands south and west of Sumatra, cut off from the 20th century influences by treacherous currents and strong winds and their out-of-the-way location are just beginning to emerge from the past. Harry Kawilarang, an acquaintance from Jakarta who has roamed his country extensively as a journalist for respected publications like *Mutiara* magazine, told me his 1976 visit to the Mentawai Islands, south of Padang, was the most remarkable of his career: "The people of Mentawai are the original flower people. They were still dressing in banana leaves and bark cloth. Women gave birth naturally in the rivers. I found them to be peaceful and happy living with their traditions and in no hurry to change."

On Nias island, north of the Mentawai group, there are vestiges of a megalithic Stone Age culture. The 140-kilometer by 50-kilometer island is peppered with stone obelisks and monoliths reminiscent of the famous statues on Easter Island in the Pacific. Whole villages are paved with flat slabs and many have stone stairways and sculptured gateways. The ancient village of Baawomataluo, built on a hill at the top of four flights of stairs, 700 in all, is dominated by the palatial home of its chieftain that is raised on a forest of wooden pilings and has a roof 23 meters above the flagstones. Two polished black funerary tablets in front of the mega-hut were once used as the final resting place of decaying corpses. Carved reliefs of men with pronounced sexual attributes, animals and flower petals, typical of Nias-coveted art, adorn the village.

Large stone blocks cut to form terraces, walls and the foundations of some of the villages of north Sumatra, particularly in the Batak region of Lake Toba, and large flat blocks found in southeast Sumatra indicate that the Megalithic cultures like those of Nias probably existed on the main island before the arrival of Islam. Even Megalithic stone sarcophagi and anthropomorphic statues are found on Toba's Samosir Island.

Catholic and Protestant missionaries have won many converts among the half-million inhabitants of Nias, but animistic beliefs still govern many aspects of life. One resident bluntly told us that the local weather was under his command. He said he could conjure up clouds or clear skies as he wished. Another categorically claimed to control a veritable bevy of spirits. Cats are accorded special respect. The bridge to the land of the dead of Nias was believed guarded by a cat who pushed off anyone who had not made his mark as a headhunter during his lifetime — or, perhaps, who had mistreated cats.

One of the specialties of the agile men of Nias is stone jumping. We watched as a young man launched himself from an oval rock and catapulted over a truncated pyramid of stones piled more than two meters high. He easily cleared the top and landed as gracefully as a world-class gymnast. The practice is a throwback to rites of manhood and warrior training of earlier times. Back then, as an added incentive to making a successful jump, sharp bamboo spikes were added to the tops of the stone pyramids. It was all part of the physical preparation for launching an attack in the days when a warrior had to leap over the walls of enemy villages with a torch in one hand and a sword in the other.

Inevitably, the winds of change are beginning to reach the distant shores of Nias. Young men's thoughts no longer turn only to stone jumping. When waves crash on the island's gorgeous beaches especially from June to September, blonde-haired youths from afar take to the water with flat, shiny boards in a new ritual that gives them the mysterious power to ride on the crest of the waves like gods of old.

The boat-shaped stone sarcophagus of Raja Sida Butar (above) in the village of Tomok on Samosir island in Sumatra's Lake Toba indicates the big island's culture once resembled the megalithic culture of Nias. In Nias, a young man in the village of Hilismaetano launches himself over a stone pyramid (right).

Chapter Five

Islands of the Gods

Our ubiquitous Travelers attend the grand Cremation of Cokorda Gede Agung Sukawati and a mass Exorcism of the World and discover that Bali's extraordinary Culture has survived the Onslaught of Tourists; they then cross the Channel to Lombok island which divulges the Secret of the Nyale.

A blast of hot air embraced me like an old friend when I stepped out the door of the Garuda Indonesian Airways DC–9. It was July 1978 and people already had long lamented the demise of Bali's fabled culture. Yet beyond the modern runway and neat little terminal at Ngurah Rai Airport there was little to lament. A line of taxi drivers out front were honking like a gaggle of geese when I arrived with other members of a University of Hawaii study group. A steel-framed, copper-colored young man who had been dispatched to meet us, loaded our luggage into the trunk of a '63 Dodge Polara. On its dashboard was a palm leaf heaped with flowers and other tidbits meant to placate the god in charge of the island's highways. It would be suicidal to venture into Bali's treacherous traffic without divine aegis.

Thus we drove off into this paramount paradise of Indonesia's myriad paradises, past kelly-green *padi* fields, enchanting temple and residential compounds, over bridges guarded by sculptured stone gods and rivers running with children and women scrubbing clothes. Along the roadsides, men squatted in sarongs and caressed brawny fighting cocks. Young women with irresistible smiles sat in shacks selling cigarettes, bags of peanuts, bottles of pastel-colored liquids and packets of Rinso. While rounding one bend, our driver punched the horn, then veered sharply to avoid several chickens and three sun-browned women. Each somehow kept a bulky sheaf of rice balanced on her head. I turned and was stunned to find them all elderly in spite of their athletic gaits. The bare flat breasts of one flopped limply as she bobbed up and down under her load.

The charming dioramas of Balinese life flashed past until we turned into a dusty lane and drove up to the impressive, decaying walls of the palace of Puri Saren in the village of Ubud. We stopped in front of a gate, an immense stone monolith about nine meters tall topped by a series of roofs, each smaller than the one below. It looked like an old Polaroid camera that had been pulled out of its flat case and laid on its back. Two statues of club-toting creatures with grisly faces guarded the gate. The menacing figures wore black-and-white checked sarongs around their waists. Did the Balinese believe these stone gods lived and breathed?

We walked past the statues into a courtyard surrounded by more walls. It led to yet another passageway. The visage of a monster with wings in place of ears glared stonily from above the portal. Beyond was an overgrown courtyard and more stone figures and cozy bungalows that were to be our accommodation for the week. The decor in the bungalows could only be described as "early grass hut". There were no modern amenities. Mosquito nets hung over simple, but very comfortable beds. Kerosene lamps primed for darkness stood on tables. The daily water supply was delivered each morning by another man who fetched it from a nearby well and poured it into a square tiled basin through a hole in the bathroom wall. We bathed in traditional style — by holding our breaths and dumping scoops of cold water over our heads. We slept in traditional style — jarred in and out of dreams and nightmares by the echoing, stentorian "tuck-koo, tuck-koo, tuck-koo" of tokay lizards, waking to the "craw-craw-crawww" of cocks.

Our host at the compound was to be Cokorda Gede Agung Sukawati, one of the last of the island's royal leaders and the impetus behind Bali's artistic renaissance. With the help of European artists like

Bali's fabled Uluwatu, a temple compound carved out of solid coral on the edge of a sheer cliff 100 meters above the ocean (preceding pages), cuts a mystical silhouette against the setting sun. A Balinese beauty (left) dons an ornate, hand-tooled headdress embellished with flowers as she prepares for a ritual dance.

A procession of gaily-attired Balinese women display a keen sense of balance as they quickstep to a temple carrying bowls stacked tall with rice cakes, fruit, flowers and other offerings. Religious festivals occur somewhere almost every day, making the island a neverending carnival of color, music, dance, drama and feasting.

Walter Spies and Rudolf Bonnet who had settled in Bali, the Cokorda had formed a group known as Pita Maha in 1935 for the purpose of teaching and inspiring local painters, woodcarvers, sculptors, silversmiths and weavers. It enabled the creative heritage of a few aging individuals to be passed on, absorbed and ultimately expanded upon by legions of new young artists. Word of the Cokorda's art colony made him an international celebrity and he entertained guests like Charlie Chaplin, Marlon Brando, Ho Chi Minh, the King and Queen of Holland and Robert Kennedy in the very same bungalows. Unfortunately, the Cokorda was not there to enthrall us with tales of his encounters with legendary celebrities and of Ubud and Bali's artistic renaissance, as he was so fond of doing.

In fact, the grounds of Puri Saren seemed peculiarly abandoned and devoid of life during our stay, except for the stone statues and hideous old wooden masks that hung on the verandas of some of the bungalows. Inert in the daylight, their countenances seemed to come terrifyingly alive with emotion when the beam of a flashlight or pressure lamp played on their tortured features at night. Perhaps it was just my imagination, over-activated by stories of Bali's vampires and witches. But a few days after we left Ubud, I learned that the old Cokorda, whose spirit had become part of Puri Saren and all that surrounded it, had been ill in a hospital in Surabaya. He had died the very week we had stayed at his palace. The Cokorda's death at the age of 73 set in motion one of the most spectacular events in the history of the island.

Bali is the best known of Indonesia's islands, romanticized in travelogues, fiction and film. There are bits and pieces of it in James Michener's imaginary Bali Hai. Balinese art has been compared to the work of Aubrey Beardsley and Hieronymus Bosch. Its festivals and music have inspired contemporary pop stars like David Bowie and Jon Anderson. "Bali goes its own peculiar way, a land that has no struggle for existence," wrote American journalist Hickman Powell during a visit in the 1920s.

The island is compressed into 5,623 square kilometers, half that of Jamaica in the West Indies, but encompasses an amazing number of idyllic vistas. It is doubtful any of the world's islands boast

of a view like the one from the ridge in the village of Sayan of emerald rice field terraces, of a silver river that foams as it tumbles over boulders at the bottom of a profound ravine and of the sapphire silhouettes of a distant volcano range. It is absolutely sublime, especially in the morning and evening when flocks of herons float through the gorge in the orchid sunrise and crimson sunset.

Bali, like much of Indonesia, is at its best at times of transition. When rice planting begins and harvest ends, the villages swirl with feasting and dancing and the hypnotic cadences of the gamelan. When human life begins, an infant is carried everywhere until its first birthday, by Balinese reckoning 210 days later, to spare him the shame of crawling like an animal. When children become young adults, their teeth are filed with great fanfare to reduce the evils of human nature (greed, anger, jealousy, etc.) and decrease the chance of human error and frailty. And, when life ends, crowds of sarong-clad men hoist on their shoulders palm tree-high funerary towers festooned with the garish, bug-eyed creatures of Balinese myth and send the spirit of the deceased to the afterlife on a fiery pyre. Religion governs every phase of life in Bali.

These transitions are not in the least bit subtle. For instance, at the end of the year and the beginning of a new one by Bali's lunar calendar, on a day called *Nyepi*, beaches and temples and streets empty out and an eerie, uncharacteristic stillness descends on the island. People stay home and refrain from lighting fires and from working, in an effort to trick mischief-making evil spirits into abandoning the island by making them believe it is devoid of life. Colin McPhee wrote of Bali's transitionary moods in his lyrical *A House in Bali*:

"In the early morning the island had a golden freshness, dripped and shone with moisture like a garden in a florist's window. By noon it had become hard and matter-of-fact. But in the late afternoon the island was transformed once more; it grew unreal, lavish and theatrical like old-fashioned opera scenery. As the sun neared the horizon men and women turned the color of new copper, while shadows grew purple, the grass blue, and everything white reflected a deep rose."

McPhee was a young American composer who spent several years studying Balinese music during the creative frenzy of the 1930s. He built his house on the ridge at Sayan tucked away from the main tourist tracks of Bali's populous southeast. Most of the island's three million people live in close-knit

villages on the southeastern and south central slopes of the island, an area dominated by the island's tallest mountain, 3,142-meter Mt. Agung. Usually shrouded by clouds and always cloaked in mystery, Agung is the home of Bali's Supreme God, Sanghyang Widi Wasa, in His manifestations as Brahma, Visnu and Siva, the triumvirate of the Hindu religion. He dwells there alongside the island's ancient spirits which, according to traditional texts etched on strips of *lontar* palm, include a powerful ancestor named Hyang To Langkir.

Besakih, the mother of Bali's teeming family of temples, rises in a series of terraces that resemble stone *padi* under the shadows of Agung's summit. Consisting of nearly 200 interrelated structures scattered around the mountain's slopes, Besakih is to the Balinese what the Vatican is to Catholics and the K'aabah to Muslims, the focus of worship. It contains 57 shrines, a litany in stone composed over the centuries by a succession of priests and rulers. Its altars, gates, statues, storehouses and pavilions all play a role in the complex rituals of Bali's distinctive form of Hinduism.

Less important in the temple hierarchy, but equally breathtaking to behold, is Tanah Lot. Built on an outcropping licked by rolling breakers off a promontory on the southwest shore, it can be reached on foot at low tide, and temple processions through the surf and creamy seas have always inspired artists and photographers. Guides take visitors into the caves in the cliffs near the temple and by the light of lanterns point out coiled snakes, the guardians of Tanah Lot.

Bali's temples are both the inspiration and the setting for the fabled festivals that bring the somber gray stones to life with their color and movement. Women in form-fitting *sarong kebaya* balance stacks of plates and bowls filled with fruit, flowers and rice cakes on their heads and parade on dikes and paths through *padi* and forest to temple ceremonies. Men with scarves twisted around their heads carry gamelan instruments. Others prance in the costumes of the good Barong, a bizarre hybrid creature, and its arch-enemy, the witch Rangda, a weird striped vampire with tusks, fangs, bulging ebony eyes and bouncing breasts. Temples are sometimes the scene of morality plays that depict violent battles between these forces of good and evil, played out in dance and drama, that rapidly build in intensity until some of the actors snap into trances. With glazed eyes, they gyrate spastically and try to impale themselves on the points of their kris daggers. Inexplicably, the blades rarely penetrate their skin, an enigma the Balinese attribute to the powers of the Barong.

Nearly 40 per cent of Indonesia's population is under the age of 15 and children are highly visible on crowded Bali. Children go for a stroll on the beach as a fleet of *perahu* return from fishing (left) or frolic on the beach (above) with a fish-shaped kite.

Extraordinary spectacle is routine in Bali. Pilgrims from India who visited the island centuries ago called the island *Wali*, the Sanskrit word for religious festival. Even today few days pass without them. Within only two months in 1983 I attended rites at Tanah Lot where stands of *penjor*, tall bamboo poles, and banners fluttered above the multiple rooftops while high priests, garbed in white cloaks, chanted mantras and burned incense to wooden deities painted in pastel greens, yellows, reds and blues. I motorcycled up to the temple at Uluwatu, which is carved out of solid coral on the edge of a sheer 100 meter cliff, past whole families loaded with offerings who walked uphill for miles to worship there. I went to a village near Klungkung where hundreds gathered at an ancient temple, and joined in their procession through the jungle, down steep cliffs to the rocky shallows of a river where offerings were made. Then I followed them back as night blackened the clearing in front of the temple where young men walked with empty palanquins on which spirits "sat down" and carried them into violent, dizzying charges around and around, like men possessed. And I went to Kesiman as a guest of the village's royal family at a festival in which seven Barong teams and seven Rangda from neighboring villages came to life dancing and jousting with each other and sent young boys into violent kris-wielding trances. Pop star David Bowie, who happened to be vacationing on the island at the time, recorded their supernatural antics for one of his music videos.

Balinese music and dance have themes, movements and melodies similar to those of Java but are usually faster-paced and more sprightly. Hugh Mabbett in his book *The Balinese*, quotes Charlie Chaplin who perfectly summed up the different styles: "The Javanese dance the Idea, the Balinese dance the Action."

Perhaps the most classic of all Balinese dances is the graceful *Legong*, in which a pair of prepubescent girls twist and turn their bodies into impossible position in unison to music. Then there is the mystifying *Sanghyang Dedari*, the "dance of the revered angels," in which two nubile girls who had never danced before fall into trances and match each other in a series of complex legong movements — with their eyes closed! It's magic, say the Balinese, and it is hard to argue with that explanation.

A Balinese funeral is a compendium of music, art and ritual. The auspicious day set for the Cokorda's cremation occurred on January 31, 1979. His body had been preserved in special fluids and herbs and kept at the palace for six months while the expensive preparations were being made. Thousands of people from Ubud and other villages were involved. They swept the town clean, constructed new accommodations and stockpiled food and beverages for the thousands of Indonesian and foreign guests that had been invited. A pyre was constructed at a cemetery on the village outskirts and offerings were made.

The nights leading up to the cremation moved with music and dance. A high priest purified everything with water blessed by the recitation of mantras, esoteric gestures and the ringing of bells. Elaborate offerings included a severed water buffalo head draped with a necklace of old Chinese coins, a special gift to welcome the important ancestral deities that were expected to drop in for the cremation. Meanwhile, craftsmen fashioned a 20 meter-tall tower, a bamboo-and-rattan gridwork topped with nine thatched roofs, only one roof removed from the rank of a god. It was decorated front and back with the face of Bhoma, a monster with a menacing overbite, and the tinsel-covered

wings and toothy beak of Garuda, the half-human bird of local myth. The tower blocked a road outside the walls of Puri Saren. A ramp connected one of its highest compartments with the palace grounds.

I made a special trip to Bali to cover the cremation. This time the driver had to park miles from the village. I walked in through hordes of people and found sleepy Ubud had been transformed into a carnival of activity. Even an electrical generator had been installed in the palace. Newspapers estimated the crowd at 100,000. Three European television stations sent camera crews. The Balinese roared with laughter as they watched foreigners risk their necks climbing up palm trees for a better view. Others, like good capitalists everywhere, saw the opportunity to profit from the event. They hawked drinks and souvenirs at high prices. Some constructed bamboo viewing platforms. A fat man in a yellow sarong, white shirt and dark sunglasses was the proprietor of one row of box seats. "That one rents for 15,000 rupiahs or US$25 cash. Last price," he said. He got his price.

At the appointed time, a siren sounded and a gamelan began banging out a marching beat. The Cokorda's body, swathed in white silk, was carried up the ramp by his sons and two of them stayed with it precariously perched high above the ground.

Then hundreds of men clambered under the tower and hoisted it on their shoulders, orchestra and all. The crowd roared its approval. The tower was turned around three times to confuse the Cokorda's spirit so it would not be able to find its way back to the palace. The spirit had not been freed of its earthly bonds and would try to cling to temporal things.

The Agung's sons held tight to the body — and the tower — during a harrowing ride high above sheer cliffs that flanked the road. The tower tilted and dipped precariously. But the wiry carriers never collapsed under its weight. The glittering catafalque floated on a sea of gaily-dressed men and women huddled under colored parasols. Several European relatives of Rudolf Bonnet carried a large photograph of the painter and an urn containing some of his ashes in the procession. Bonnet had passed away in Holland the year before the death of the Cokorda. His last wish was that his own ashes accompany those of his royal friend on their journey to paradise.

When the procession reached the burial grounds, the tower was placed alongside another ramp that had been constructed there. Relatives helped the weary weak-kneed sons out of the tower and down the ramp, then passed the corpse down. The Cokorda's body was placed in the bowels of a big black bull made from bamboo and paper. The bull

A winged dragon-like creature (above), fashioned from wood and paper to symbolically transport the ashes of Dutch painter Rudolf Bonnet to heaven, is carried to the cremation grounds during the funeral rites held for Cokorda Gede Agung Sukawati in Ubud on January 31, 1979. A stone relief of a *pemangku*, a village priest (left), is carved into a temple facade.

was correct to the very last detail — a mighty mechanized pink erection that had elicited waves of laughter during the procession. There is a thin line between the sacred and the profane in Bali. The ashes and photograph of Bonnet were placed in a winged dragon-like creature. Then all these artistic masterpieces were set ablaze. The Balinese are well aware that art, like life, is temporary. The conflagration popped and crackled and its intense heat forced the crowds back into the trees. A few of the viewing platforms collapsed under the weight of spectators vying for a look. Finally, the charred corpse crashed through the burning stomach of the bull and the smoke carried the spirit of the Cokorda to heaven.

It is true that there has not been a cremation on the scale of the Agung's since. It is also true that since the late seventies new hotels around the tourist enclaves of Kuta and Sanur and a government-built enclave called Nusa Dua have brought more tourism and commercialism to the island. Gamelan music is amplified at some performances. Young men "kidnap" their brides aboard the pillion of their motorcycles. One of the outstanding traits of the eclectic Balinese is that they adapt to change, but they have not let it swallow them or their culture.

Consider the solemn day of *Nyepi*. Hotels advise tourists to stay on the grounds of the hotel lest they be chased from the beach by religious police wearing black-and-white checkered sarongs. Indeed, every day in Bali offerings to the gods — flowers, water and specks of rice — are unfailingly laid out at concrete curbsides each morning and dogs still wander around nibbling at them. During holidays, when even Kuta and Sanur pulsate with pageantry, Balinese dress in their best. Some outfits are amalgams of local formal wear and Western T-shirts or jeans. Holy services are held on beaches amidst oiled tourists clad only in G-strings, carrying surfboards, playing paddle ball and buying soft drinks and souvenirs from peddlers.

Bali is still Bali and nearly a solid century of gawking tourists has not diminished its rich culture. If anything, tourism has pumped more life into the cultural rebirth nurtured by the Cokorda and his contemporaries. Although the vast majority of wood carvings, paintings and "antiques" passed off on visitors is strictly mass-produced souvenir stuff, there are probably more outstanding artists and craftsmen in Bali today than at any time in its history. The superb work of stalwarts like Budi of Batuan and of carvers like Ida Bagus Nyana and his son Ida Bagus Tilem of Mas command high prices around the world. Village dance companies and gamelan orchestras, with the welcome infusion of dollars from tourist performances, have been able to afford brand new costumes and instruments that inspire them to take as much pride as ever in their art.

The innate, simmering creativity of the Balinese has found renewed vigor and new outlets. Demand for colorful, lightweight clothing by the colonies of young people who plant their bodies on its beaches each year has given rise to a blossoming fashion industry on the island. Boutiques, crammed with original designs and imitations that are better than the Japanese originals, have attracted the attention of entrepreneurs from around the world. While in Legian Beach, I once met a German who was buying clothes from the Balinese and selling them to shops in Jamaica — a country that has its own colorful clothing traditions.

Ubud was charming but shabby and in need of a facelift when I first visited. After the palace was renovated for the Cokorda's funeral, many temples and housing compounds were also repaired and cleaned up and the village has begun looking like an idyll, the way its poetic painters would have you believe it should. Ponds of drifting lotus pads dress up the gates of the Saraswati temple. Visitors can sip espresso at the pleasant Lotus Cafe while taking in the scenery. On the outskirts of town, Murni's Warung serves up plates of fried rice or the all American Upper Elk Valley cheeseburger and overlooks the picturesque gorge where Walter Spies built his artist's retreat. The constant influx of visitors has given the people of Ubud and elsewhere reason to be proud of their villages and to spruce them up and keep them tidy. Bali's ubiquitous dogs are still ugly, but even they at least look healthier.

Those who decry the landscaping, the espresso, crocheted bikinis and airbrushed T-shirts do not have an inkling what Bali is all about. As Spies and Beryl de Zoete noted in their classic *Dance and Drama in Bali*, the "suppleness of mind" that the Balinese possess "has enabled them to take what they want of the alien civilizations which have been reaching them for centuries and to leave the rest."

The funeral tower that carried the remains of Cokorda Gede Agung Sukawati collapses in flames. Minutes later, the inferno consumed a black bamboo-and-wood bull that contained the body of the beloved Cokorda. Spectacular cremations are an important part of Bali's legendary culture that have survived change.

A Balinese farmer hikes home with a huge hoe in hand after a
day of hard work in a *padi*. Terraced wet rice fields complement
much of Bali's mountainous terrain in such a picturesque manner
that the entire island is a veritable work of art.

Resilience to inevitable change has been an important trait of the Balinese throughout their history. Recorded history begins around the year 1000 A.D when King Airlangga was in control in East Java. According to an American Baliphile, Willard A. Hanna, Airlangga's father was a Balinese king with the extravagant name Dharmmodayananwarmmadewa. His mother was a Javanese queen with a more modest name, Gunapriyadharmapatni, or Mahendradatta for short. Airlangga appointed a relative to rule Bali, thus beginning close contacts between the nobility of the two neighboring islands.

In spite of the contacts, Bali always managed to maintain a great degree of autonomy from its big sister island. The line of local leaders used a title that implied they ruled by divine right, independent of Java — Dewa Agung, the Great Deity. The first great Dewa Agung was Batu Renggong. According to Hanna, he "achieved previously undreamed of splendor and authority." Batu Renggong built a strong centralized kingdom and conquered and colonized Lombok. Hanna said he also created "the contemporary Balinese culture" from the legacy of East Java's Majapahit Empire. "It is the riddle and the miracle of Bali that from the embers of Majapahit Java should have been ignited the fires which still burn bright in the neighboring isle," wrote Hanna.

Europeans arrived in the 16th century, first the Portuguese then the Dutch. It was during the first Dutch expedition in 1598 that two sailors, Jacob Claaszoon and Emanuel Roodenburg decided Bali had more to offer than Holland, jumped ship, married Balinese women and went to work for the Dewa Agung. Other foreigners also came and stayed. A flamboyant Danish trader, Mads Lange, set up shop in Kuta in 1839 and later died and was buried there. Lange wheeled-and-dealed, often acting as an intermediary in the feuding and warring between the Dutch and Bali's rajas.

The Balinese stubbornly maintained their independence from the Dutch until a series of tragedies occurred at the beginning of the 20th century. The Dutch, frustrated over not gaining a foothold on the island, used a lame excuse, the plundering of a shipwreck off Sanur, to send in a military force in 1904. Rather than surrender, the Raja of Denpasar put on ceremonial white robes, summoned his family and had a high priest plunge his jeweled kris into his breast before the stunned Dutch troops. The Raja's family and subjects followed him in ritual suicide. The mass, defiant suicide is called the *puputan*, Balinese for "the end." Four years later the Dewa Agung of Klungkung, the traditional leader of the entire island, led hundreds of his subjects in a *puputan* after coming under attack from Dutch artillery and infantry. Bali finally became an official part of the Dutch East Indies, but Balinese guerrillas fought valiantly during the war that earned Indonesia its independence.

The biggest, most dramatic event in Bali's recent history occurred after the Cokorda's funeral. Before a month had lapsed, the people of the island were preparing for what was undoubtedly the biggest traditional event in island history, a spiritual cleansing called Eka Dasa Rudra, the feast of the "eleven howlers", a violent god that in its multiple manifestations infests all 11 directions in the Balinese cosmos. The ambitious ceremonies would not only exorcise Bali of evil, but the entire world. When the Balinese do something, they do it big.

Having neglected to hold the ceremony for several centuries, the Balinese staged a scaled-down version in 1963, prior to the actual end of their century, spurred on by concern over such calamitous events as World War II, the Indonesian Revolution, a rat plague and the crash of a Pan American airliner on the island. But as the preparations for the climactic sacrifices were being made at Besakih in February, 1963, Mt. Agung erupted. Lava poured out, cutting paths of destruction. More than 2,500 people died.

Blaming the disaster on high priests who had angered the gods with half-hearted ceremonies, the Balinese were determined to pull off the ceremony without a hitch in 1979, the year 1900 by local *Saka* timetables. Rules of conduct were followed to the letter even though they required the mass sacrifice of hundreds of birds, animals and insects. High priests even pronounced the death sentence on a lovely silver eagle, an endangered species, to the dismay of naturalists. In one integral act leading up to the appointed day, priests trudged up to the rim of Agung and pushed a cow and a goat into the crater to appease its fiery gods. Other priests hiked down to the coast in a procession that grew to thousands and drowned two buffalos in the sea as an offering to its spirits and safeguard against tidal waves.

I arrived at the peak of the proceedings. By then, most of the island's three million people were making pilgrimages to Besakih on foot to pray, make offerings and join in the dancing and feasting. A special enclosure composed of altars to the 11 directions draped with banners of black, blue, white, green, red and yellow was being constructed. Temple etiquette required me to dress, like the Balinese, in a sarong with a half-skirt and sash tied around the middle and a bandana headcovering. Dozens of foreign journalists, photographers (including Kal Muller), camera crews and sound engineers clumsily stumbled about in that attire like young girls trying out their mother's high heels.

The crowd at Besakih on the day of exorcism numbered a quarter million by some estimates. They included President Suharto and his wife, Madame Tien, Muslims whose attendance exemplified the nations's religious tolerance. Despite the mass of people and the excitement, a deafening hush came over the mountainside when 23 Brahmin priests began ringing bells and chanting hymns to drive the demons from every corner of the earth.

The gruesome animal sacrifices had occurred the preceding day. Some 60 varieties of wildlife, from buffalos, horses and monkeys to centipedes and snakes, had been rounded up in a part of the complex that the foreign media were calling "God's Kitchen." All were ritually executed. Men slit the throats of the larger animals and let them bleed to a painful death. The sacrifices were not carried out maliciously. The Balinese consider the animals martyrs for a crucial cause. The pieces of some of the animals were glorified in veritable works of art. I came upon one "sculpture" fashioned from the pieces of a dismembered boar, its severed head with its tongue curled and pegged to the front, its entrails strung on skewers behind. Bizarre but ingenious.

The regal eagle, dubbed Garuda, had become a celebrity of sorts in light of its impending execution. The host of an Australian documentary even conducted an interview with the keeper of the handsome bird while the eagle, perched on his arm proudly held its head for the cameras. Minutes later, two men held the bird's long, classic wings, another clenched its tail and a fourth slit its throat and drained it of blood. They carved the bird into 108 pieces representing the essences of life.

A Balinese audience looks on in rapt attention as a royal character in a mask dance makes his appearance from behind a makeshift curtain. Such all-night performances lit by pressure lamps are still a part of daily life in Bali, whether they are held during small village festivals or as part of huge island-wide rituals like Eka Dasa Rudra.

During the festivities and work that surround the harvest on Bali's sister island of Lombok, a woman winnows rice in the field. In a manner passed down through the generations she flings up a golden mound, catches the grain on a split bamboo tray and lets the chaff fall to the ground. Rice is the focus of many rituals.

Although Bali is separated from Lombok by deep seas and Wallace's zoogeographical line, the two islands have cultural and historical links, as well as physical similarities. Lombok, east of Bali, is slightly smaller at 4,595 square kilometers. But, like Bali, its shape and spiritual essence flows from a volcano, Mt. Rinjani, which at 3,726 kilometers is taller than Mt. Agung. In the north where there are verdant forests and terraced *padi* on Rinjani's slopes and in the west where there are hundreds of Hindu temples, the resemblance to Bali — sans the hordes of tourists, hotels, cafes, fashion emporiums and discos — is obvious. The connection harks back to the 13th century when Lombok, mainly inhabited by an animistic ethnic group known as the Sasaks, was absorbed into East Java's Majapahit Empire. Bali under Batu Renggong staked its claim to Lombok in the 16th century. However, it was the Raja of East Bali's Karangasem clan which conquered Lombok in 1740 who left the most lasting influence.

The religious festivals so common in Bali also color life in the villages and countryside around Cakranegara, Ampenan and the capital of Lombok, Mataram. Also reminiscent of Bali are the fanciful gardens and bathing pools of the summer palace built in Narmada in 1805 by Anak Agung Gede Karangasem and Batu Bolong, a temple atop a large rock from which beautiful virgins were once cast into the frothing waters as offerings to the gods of the sea. The sacrifice of virgins was once a distinctly Balinese trademark.

Where the Balinese influences come up against those of the Sasaks, who practice a form of Islam flavored by generous dollops of Hinduism and animism, some peculiar practices have resulted. In Lingsar, north of Narmada, Hindus and Muslims alike gather at Pura Kemalik, a Balinese temple compound, on the night of the full moon in the sixth month of the Balinese calendar for a "rice cake war." To the tom-tomming of the *kul-kul* drums people of both faiths gather on the lower terraces of the temple and begin pelting each other with *ketupat*, rice cakes steamed in plaited palm wrappers. The melee is either designed to bring rain and insure a good harvest or to thank the gods for the last good rain and harvest, depending on whom you talk to. Some of Lombok's Muslims, in addition to traditional religious leaders like the imam and the mullah, also retain the services of a *pemangku* for decidedly non-Islamic tasks that involve the worship of the deities and spirits that inhabit the island's trees, mountains, boulders and other inanimate objects. They believe in the magic of talismans, old kris, masks, puppets, gamelan and other heirlooms.

This amalgam of religious practices in Lombok is called *Islam Wetu Telu* or *Islam Waktu Tiga*, literally "three times Muslims." By some interpretations, the label refers to the fact that some of the island's Muslims only pray on three occasions — every Friday, the Muslim holy day; on Idul Fitri, the festive day that ends the solemn fasting month of Ramadan; and on the Prophet Muhammad's birthday. Orthodox Muslims pray five times a day. Another interpretation of *Islam Waktu Tiga* came from a guide named Salim who led Kal through bone-chilling rains to the summit of Rinjani. "We have, besides our sacred Islam, the faith of our forefathers whose spirits live on Gunung Rinjani and around the lake. When the Balinese conquered our island, we also took their religion, Hinduism, which taught us to meditate in order to enter into the world of the spirits. Later, when Islam showed us the true faith, we still kept some of our former beliefs, although we know that there is no God but Allah and His prophet is Muhammad," Salim said in explaining the co-existence of three religions. About 95 per cent of Lombok's 1.5-million people consider themselves Muslims. The *Waktu Tiga* generally reside in the remote villages. The *Waktu Lima*, "five times Muslims," are concentrated in the island's population centers and central plains.

Southern and central Lombok are different physically, as well as culturally, from the northwest and from Bali. Under Rinjani, the damp mountains flatten into dry savanna that exhibits the flora and fauna characteristic of Wallacea, the lands east of Sir Alfred's boundary line between the plant and animal species of Asia and Oceania. Cotton is grown in these drier areas, then handspun into the fine weavings for which this part of Indonesia is world famous. However, much of Lombok is dominated by the cultivation of rice. Padi fields of deep emerald or rich gold are particularly abundant in the wetter areas. They are tended daily throughout the year, plowed in one place, planted with seedlings in another, and harvested somewhere else by rows of girls in big woven hats who slice off the tips of stalks with small knives in a ritual manner.

Another reminder of Bali, if only in name, is Kuta Beach on the gold-dusted southern fringe of Lombok. Thankfully devoid of Bali's holiday bungalows, the beach is also known as Putri Nyale after a preposterous wormy sea creature that washes ashore each year. The Nyale takes its names from a local folktale about Princess Mandalika Nyale, the daughter of King Berberu. Every prince on the island was captivated by the beauty of Nyale and when it came time for her to choose a husband she invited interested suitors to come to the beach. So many men turned up, Princess Nyale was unable to make a choice. Despondent, she jumped into the sea and, so the story goes, was transformed into the strange creature that haunts Kuta Beach.

The poignant story of Princess Nyale is recalled during a mass matchmaking party that usually occurs in February each year. Fires are built on Kuta Beach where unmarried young men and women are permitted the rare opportunity of mixing. The boys serenade the girls at night by the light of the bonfires with *pantun* — rhymed couplets popular throughout Indonesia and Malaysia that are romantic, even erotic — in a kind of literary competition for their affections. The words of some of the *pantun*, translated in Wilfred T. Neill's *Twentieth Century Indonesia*, reveal the passion that fuels this young nation and fires its fecundity:

> Smoke of fire, drip of dew
> At the bow of the boat, the upright
>   punt-pole thrust in.
> A heartfelt wish: that we shall never part;
> But who indeed knows Allah's will.

Merrymaking continues until the next morning when the girls set out to sea in outriggers to catch Nyale for the feasting, with the young men, like young men everywhere, in pursuit of their dreams.

> A jewel falls deep into the grass;
> Fallen in grass, it keeps on sparkling.
> Love's likeness: a dewdrop on the
>   tip of a grass blade.
> At sunrise, sure to vanish.

Columns of men and women bearing bundles of harvested rice lashed to the ends of bamboo poles are a common sight on the backroads of some Indonesian islands. The rice stalks are stored in granaries like this one in Lombok that are designed to protect the precious grain from rodents and other foraging animals.

Chapter Six

Of Warriors, Dragons and Whalers

*Stepping out from behind his Lenses, the Photographer
passes a gruesome trial-by-chicken Test on the Island of
Sumba, relates the Story of his Escape from
the Jaws of a Dragon, joins a Crew of Whalers
and discovers other bizarre Customs and
interesting Sights in the Lesser Sundas.*

Two men peered intently into a wooden bowl brimming with the blood of a chicken whose throat Kal had just slit with a dull knife. Suddenly, one of the men smiled and spat a torrent of local words at Potty, the guide. Potty translated the augury into Indonesian. "The omen is good. The feathers which have fallen in the blood are correctly aligned!"

As the group gazed at the coagulating fluid by the light of a flickering oil lamp, Kal began to look relieved — until Potty told him there were still two more tests he must pass. Then a thin but sinewy man yanked a bunch of tail feathers from the chicken's carcass and began counting them out and laying them on the ground two-by-two.

"They must come out even to show that the spirits that came with you will pair off and get along with the ancestral spirits who live here," Potty explained.

Kal held his breath and anxiously rooted for the fraternity and equality of spirits. Suspenseful minutes later, the last feathers counted out in an even pair. He had passed the second test!

Finally, a priest fished out some of that poor chicken's viscera, stuck two feathers into the oozing mess and displayed it triumphantly. The pools of tension hanging in the humid air evaporated. The silence collapsed into genial chatter. Potty reached for the feathers and coil of intestine and pointed to a floppy part. "You see the flap is open. This means that the spirits allow their descendants to welcome you and that your visit here will be successful."

"Pictures," Kal said. "What about pictures?"

Potty grinned, "*Boleh, boleh*!," he said. "You are permitted to take all the photographs you want."

Patience, persistence, a sense of adventure and, at times, even a strong stomach were essential during our travels in Indonesia. These qualities served us in particularly good stead in the more remote parts of the archipelago where people have not been conditioned by busloads of Western visitors and their idiosyncrasies. Of paramount importance in such places is the ability to respect the prevailing culture, no matter how strange some of its conventions might seem, and to be prepared for almost anything. Granted, the eviscerated chicken test administered on the island of Sumba proved a bit much even for Kal whose years as a photographer included "land-diving" in Vanuatu from the 17-meter level of a tower with only vines attached to his ankles to break his fall. Not only did such feats win him the respect of his photographic subjects, they enabled him to better understand their cultures.

I, too, was conditioned for the unexpected in Indonesia by years of searching for stories and experiences. The willingness to stick out our necks often produced unexpectedly pleasing benefits and on the strength of enduring the case of the chicken-vivisection ritual, Kal was invited to return to Sumba the following year to witness one of Indonesia's most thrilling and dangerous spectacles — the *Pasola*.

Traditions passed on from ancient generations in many parts of Indonesia call for blood to be shed, one of the best means of placating evil spirits and ensuring good weather and good harvests. Some warriors drank the blood of slain foes to obtain their *semangat*, or life force. The use of pigs, goats and water buffalos long ago replaced human sacrifices in the islands, but there are places in out-of-the-way corners, like the Lesser Sundas, where the spilling of human blood still occurs, usually by accident, sometimes by design.

A fishing vessel glides past Sumbawa (preceding pages) as the equatorial sun sets over Bima Bay. A water buffalo race on Sumbawa (left) not only provides sport and entertainment for the islanders but takes the hard work and monotony out of plowing a muddy *padi* before rice-planting begins in earnest.

On Flores, in the heart of the chain, for instance, young men engage in combat with braided water buffalo skin whips. Protected only by shields, also fashioned from the hides of water buffalos, and plenty of cloth wrapped around the head, the men lash their whips at each other. The strokes often leave deep scars and freak deaths occasionally have occurred when a jugular has been severed. Such ritualistic battles are played out at weddings and during other milestone occasions.

On Sumbawa, a large parched land of savannas and mountains east of Lombok, young men go at it with clumps of rice stalks clenched in their fists. To the admiring glances of pretty female spectators, two groups glare at each other until the mood strikes and one of the youths rips off his shirt and shows off his muscles and lissom movements with a taunting dance that coaxes an opponent from the other side to challenge him. Usually, an adversary responds with a dance of his own. After two men, who act as referees of sorts, remove the opponents' watches and rings and make sure they are not concealing stones in their fists, the beatings begin. Wild, roundhouse punches from right and left field, usually way off the mark, occasionally connect with resounding, skin-splitting whacks. After exchanging a few volleys, the adversaries confront each other toe-to-toe, trading blow-for-blow. Defensive posturings are non-existent. The referees who try to pry the pair apart often intercept a few wild punches aimed at no one in particular.

According to Mustakim, an unofficial guide from the Sumbawa cultural office, "magic" plays a predominant role in traditional boxing, known as *berempuk*, and in water buffalo races held on the island which are similar to the bull races of Madura. A *sanro*, the equivalent of a medicine man, recites powerful incantations and administers mysterious herbal preparations that enable even a man with a slight build to defeat the village behemoth. Prior to the thundering buffalo races, a team's *sanro* rubs the animals with secret oils and chants powerful mantras.

"These farmers, although good Muslims, still follow many of the ancient traditions and beliefs," said Mustakim. "They learn their prayers in Arabic and attend services at the mosque, but for many things they rely on their *sanro*, who also considers himself a good Muslim in spite of the fact that he manipulates 'magical forces.' "

***Adat*, the traditions and customs of Indonesia,** requires a man to pay a price for the bride of his choice in many of the islands of the Lesser Sundas. A groom-to-be, wearing the formal attire of his village on the island of Lembata, carries a family heirloom – a rare ivory tusk – to his wedding as his gift to the family of the blushing bride.

The Pasola held in western Sumba harks back to the days when blood, spilled in war or ritual, was believed to appease evil spirits. The spectacle of men on horseback hurling spears at each other, sometimes with deadly accuracy, is one of the most thrilling in Indonesia. Today, the Indonesian government permits only the use of blunt spears in an effort to minimize serious injuries but accidents still happen.

Women of Sumba use bamboo shafts to pound rice in a wooden trough to loosen the grain from the stalk and chaff before winnowing. Some musicologists believe the sound the women make as they pummel the rice, rhythmically tossing the bamboo from hand-to-hand, may have given rise to the gamelan music of the islands.

Probably the most bloodcurdling of the rituals of the Lesser Sundas is the Pasola, the ancient war games held annually on Sumba island, southeast of Sumbawa. Performed as part of the days of celebrations that insure the community's good health and an abundant harvest, men from opposing villages square off against each other on horseback brandishing spears, much in the manner of tribal wars of decades past. Today, Indonesian government regulations restrict warriors to the use of blunt spears and the Pasola is largely ceremonial. But as the men thunder toward each other, their horses in full gallop, the lingering spirit of old rivalries takes over. They hurl their spears with deadly accuracy.

Fascinated by the prospect of cavalry charges that were right out of the Middle Ages, Kal took up the invitation and attended the Pasola several times. Once, he saw a Pasola rider die when a spear tore a gaping hole in his throat. While clicking away with his cameras during another visit, he watched in horror as a rider was trampled to death after being thrown from his horse.

Indonesia's Lesser Sundas, as distinguished from the Greater Sundas of Sumatra, Java, Borneo and Sulawesi, anchor a 1,400-kilometer south central corner of the Indonesian archipelago. They stretch from Bali and Lombok in the west to Alor in the east. In between are Sumbawa, Sumba, Komodo, Flores, Lembata, and even more obscure islands.

As in the Greater Sundas, Islam is the predominant religion. The most devout Muslims are those of Sumbawa. The island's Bima regency sends a higher percentage of its population on the Islamic pilgrimage to Mecca — the Haj — than any other in Indonesia. Sponsored by the government, the Haj costs the equivalent of about ten good-sized water buffalos. The conservative Islamic dress, *kerundung*, in which women cover their arms, legs, heads and even the lower parts of their faces is common in Bima. There are also large pockets of Catholics in the former Portuguese colony of East Timor and in Flores around Larantuka. But the religions are all influenced by age-old beliefs and spirit worship.

In Flores, for instances, some dwellings called *kada* house relics and heirlooms to which offerings are made. Beams in some *kada* are carved with life-sized human figures of a man and a woman which to the villagers simultaneously represent Jesus and Mary or the Sun God, the man, and Mother Earth, the female figure. On the south central part of Flores, an island which bears a resemblance to a scorpion with its tail cocked for combat, the villagers of Bajawa annually conduct a special mass known as Maha Kudu. The service is essentially Catholic, but its celebration is preceded by a deer hunt in which young women wash their hands with the blood of slain animals to enhance their fertility and followed by a procession of writhing, sword-wielding people who carry the crucifix around town. In days gone by, people were required by local custom to bury a child — alive — under the foundations of a new home under construction. And people in the mountains believed that gold that was washed in the blood of two children would multiply. Relatively pure forms of aboriginal religions persist mainly on Sumba and in eastern Timor.

Compared to crowded Java and Bali, the three provinces that comprise this part of the Lesser Sundas are sparsely-populated. They have less than 4.5 million people, not including Lombok, which together with Sumbawa makes up the province called West Nusa Tenggara. Most are of Malay racial stock, but there are increasing numbers of Melanesians as one moves east through the chain, and there is a melange of Veddoids, Negritos and Australoids in Timor and Flores, evidence of this part of the archipelago's proximity to Australia and New Guinea. Their hair is more wiry, noses are wider and flatter and skins darker than the Malays.

To a certain extent, the small populations here are also a result of the these islands' connection with Oceania. The soils, in marked contrast to Bali and the islands of the Greater Sundas, are generally poor. Much of Flores, Portuguese for "Flowers," is the antithesis of its name, arid and dusty. Timor, the largest of the Lesser Sundas islands, is rugged and barren. Timor's inability to feed its inhabitants has been compounded by the fact that its farmers are not noted for efficiency. In fact, 50 families from Bali, where the farmers all have green thumbs, have been transmigrated to East Timor in hopes that they will teach the local farmers their secrets. The impact of agriculture on population density is apparent on tiny Sawu island, not far from Timor. Sawu has the same climate and soil conditions, but is more densely populated because of the extensive planting of the *lontar* palm. Its farmers have adapted agriculture to the harsh ecology. The *lontar* takes easily to the dry soil and, when tapped, secretes a rich liquid that is the staple of the Sawunese diet, consumed directly in forms that include an alcoholic beverage and which is also fed to pigs.

The people of the Southeast Islands, as the provincial name Nusa Tenggara literally is translated, are mostly subsistence farmers. Soil-decimating slash-and-burn techniques are the norm. Cassava and yams are planted in the islands along with corn, a popular starch introduced by the Portuguese 300 years ago. Rice is grown in a few wetter areas or in flat, irrigated fields like those around Bima and Sumbawa Besar. The introduction of new miracle strains of rice requiring large doses of fertilizer has also helped boost yields — and nutritional standards — in the Lesser Sundas.

Wedged between the volatile Sunda continental shelf and the Sahul shelf, the geography of the Lesser Sundas runs the gamut from islands that have potent volcanos to those that have none whatsoever. Flores, 370 kilometers long but just 56 kilometers across at its widest point, has eight active craters. Its most well-known peak is one believed to be extinct, Keli Mutu, with its three colored lakes, one turquoise, two burgundy. The local people attribute the colors to the fate of the souls of the dead. The spirits of those who led fine, moral lives wind up in the light-colored lake while the souls of those who were evil and sinful are vanquished to the dark sinister waters. Scientists say the coloration results from acid-alkaline imbalances.

Another of Indonesia's renowned volcanos, Tambora, looms over Saleh Bay on Sumbawa. *The Guinness Book of World Records* claims that Tambora, not Krakatau, produced the most powerful and destructive natural explosion in recorded history. On April 10, 1815, the once cone-shaped mountain literally blew its top, more than 1,000 meters of it. In a matter of minutes, the 4,200-meter high mountain was reduced to just 2,820 meters and a jagged crater. About 10,000 people were killed in the initial eruption and another 75,000 died in the aftermath from starvation and disease. Another 30,000 people fled the island. Thirty-two years after the explosion, an eyewitness reported that once fer-

A young girl carries an earthen water jug on her head (top) on a ridge above the white sand and surf of a Sumba bay. A high priest of the old religion on Savu (bottom) takes a breather on a stone believed to be a sacred abode of spirits.

Indonesian tourists intent on getting good photographs edge perilously close to a family of Komodo dragons that are at least temporarily preoccupied with a meal. The dragons' inarticulated jaws open wide enough to swallow a young lamb whole. The fresh goat carcass was strung up by the guide to lure the carnivorous lizards from their lairs.

tile areas of Sumbawa were still covered with more than a half meter of volcanic debris. Sixty years later another account reported wide-spread hunger and farmers who were selling their children into slavery for three kilograms of rice.

The effects of the Australian zoogeographical connection on vegetation is readily apparent on Sumbawa and other islands in the Lesser Sundas. There is an abundance of eucalyptus and casuarina trees and *lontar* palms. The extremely poor lime-stone soils of Sumba and Timor produce sandalwood. However, there are patches of rain forest in the uplands where there is high rainfall, particularly on Flores. Expanses of useless grasslands are an indirect result of the dry climate and of shifting agricultural cultivation, the legacy of numerous bush fires that occur during the long dry season. As Wallace pointed out, the fauna is also related to that of Australia and includes marsupials from bats to the platypus and anteater. There are none of the large animals of the western islands, only smaller species. There are also reptiles.

One of the most unusual national parks in the world is centered on Komodo Island, an arid asterisk of rock between the islands of Sumbawa and Flores. Freckled with golden-green, thorny zizyphus trees and tall, fan-leafed *lontar* palms, Komodo is crawling with lizards so monstrous they are called "dragons." Komodo is a forbidding island that has changed little since the dinosaur age. It is the kind of place Kal Muller finds positively inviting. He has made no less than a half-dozen trips to the island intent on capturing the Komodo dragons on film.

Armed with razor claws, serrated teeth, toxic saliva and a powerful tailswipe, the lizards grow up to three meters long and weigh more than 100 kilograms. Their only known pastime is eating. They specialize in dismembering goats and swallowing the pieces whole. Their lethal gastric juices dissolve bone, hoof, horns, teeth, claws, hair and all.

Understandably, the local guides on Komodo get nervous if visitors begin inching within 10 meters of these inhospitable creatures. During the 1970s, several dragons reportedly dined on a Swiss tourist who made the fatal mistake of napping near their stomping grounds. All that remained of the unfortunate man were his camera and glasses.

Such unnerving stories only made the Komodo dragons a more worthy photographic subject for my impetuous colleague. Determined to get sensational shots of the dragons in action, Kal once climbed from a viewing embankment down a tree to a riverbed where six *ora*, as the locals call the dragons, were gorging on a goat — and almost ended up as dessert. Kal got his pictures, but, as he started climbing back up the tree, he turned to find that one of the monsters that apparently got shortchanged on the goat was following him with a hungry look in its eye. Kal jumped to the embankment, but the lizard easily scaled the tree and jumped after him, toxic saliva dripping from its forked tongue.

Quick thinking by the local guide rescued Kal. The guide remembered that he had retained the liver from the goat before feeding the carcass to the dragons. Pulling the raw meat out, he made sure the menacing lizard got a good whiff of the liver then tossed it into the bush. The dragon went for it without a backward glance.

Except for Flores, the Lesser Sundas are lacking in the overwhelming natural and physical beauty of many of Indonesia's other islands. Yet their diverse peoples, cultures, prized art forms and traditional ways of making a living from the land and sea still classify them as a paradise of things pristine.

The *adat* in most of the Lesser Sundas calls for payment for a bride. On Alor, the family of the groom pays with huge bronze kettle drums known as *moko*. (In a mystery archaeologists have been unable to fully explain, thousands of these ornate antique drums that originated in North Vietnam's Dong-son culture 2,000 years ago have been unearthed on tiny Alor.) The men of Lembata often exchange whole ivory tusks for brides, a prohibitive custom that has become almost exclusive to the wealthier families that can afford to keep such rare heirlooms. Mere bangles of ivory can be used as a "bride price" on Sumba and Flores. At a wedding we attended in Sumbawa, the bridegroom presented his mate's family simply with an offering of Indonesian coins and a large five franc piece that was dated 1833. In most places, the bride in return gives her groom and his family fine textiles — the much-prized *ikat* of the Lesser Sundas.

Ikat is a complex weaving process in which handspun threads are individually-colored with natural dyestuffs like turmeric, indigo and candlenut. Patterns in the warp threads are formed by tying off designated areas with dye-resistant fibers. Women then use bamboo looms to weave the dye-patterned threads into fabrics with various motifs including geometric patterns, human figures, manta rays, lizards, earring designs and ships. Like so many aspects of life in Indonesia, the design as well as the weaving process itself is strictly governed by local *adat*.

For example, a woman may be required to make offerings to the first ancestor who made such a cloth before she weaves her first piece of *ikat*. Men are strictly prohibited from touching the threads. A person's caste determines whether he or she is permitted to wear the finished product. The finest pieces have been known to take up to 10 years to complete and today command exorbitant prices among collectors throughout the world. Best known are *hinggi*, a type of shoulder wrap and sarong, produced in Sumba. Unfortunately, the demand for *ikat* among souvenir collectors has encouraged the mass production of inferior artificially-dyed pieces in recent years. On the positive side, the popularity of *ikat* has made for one of the few successful cottage industries in the Lesser Sundas, where unemployment is a problem.

Otherwise, the only products the Lesser Sundas export are cattle and coffee and to a lesser extent, onions, garlic, copra and dried fish. Many who cannot make their living from the land turn to the sea. One kind of fishing, still carried out in an age-old manner occurs on Lembata, also known as Lomblen, a small island wedged between Adonara, Solor and Pantar. Kal, in the tradition of Hemingway, subjected himself to another of those invigorating ordeals to go there and photograph it. He described it to me during a lull in our travels.

"We were dozing on coils of homemade rope on the deck of a primitive *prahu* when an excited shout woke us up. There was a sudden flurry around me where only seconds before there had been a lazy sort of tranquility. Some 200 meters off the starboard bow, a sperm whale was spitting a plume of saltwater from its blowhole.

"The crew jumped to their feet and quickly

A detail of a sample of Sumba's prized *ikat* weaving (top left) and a detail of another form of fabric fashioned from cowrie shells and beads (top right) are decorated with powerful ancestral figures. Women of Lembata (bottom) use their toes as well as their fingers to load balls of yarn onto wooden spools.

lowered the craft's large, palm-plaited sail. The men were diminutive but brown and strong. Some grabbed wooden paddles, everyone prayed, then we all urinated in unison. The boat surged toward the spot where the whale had dived beneath the waves.

"The crew chanted what to me sounded something like 'Hilabe-hilabe! Hela, Hela!' The thrill of the chase seemed to send shivers of anticipation through everyone. I aimed my camera at a muscled bald man of about 50 who mounted a platform on the prow. In his hand, he held a sharp metal harpoon set in a bamboo shaft two-and-a-half-meters long. Suddenly, the whale lunged to the surface. It spouted, drenching some of the crew.

"'He's too big for us. If we do not spear him just right, he could easily break up this boat,' one of the men told me in Indonesian. 'Perhaps if there were more boats we would try our luck but there is only one other launch out today.'

"The whale swam away through the warm equatorial waters until it disappeared. The dismayed crew stared sadly after it, then set sail for home."

Home was Lamalera on Lembata, a volcano-pocked 1,200-square-kilometer chunk of earth. For the people there, whaling has been the primary livelihood for centuries. Changing times have seen a decline in the occupation as the village's younger men have sought more rewarding jobs in other parts of Indonesia, but some of Lembata's men still pursue whales the risky old way. A death or two each hunting season is not uncommon.

According to Father Dupont, the hospitable head of a parish mission that Kal met in Lamelera on the largely Catholic island in the mid-seventies, young men consider whaling a boring activity and its days appear numbered. Kal continued his story.

"Our group set off shortly after sunrise each morning, rolling their boat *Pusaka* - 'Heirloom' - out to sea on logs, and often spent several days drifting idly under the hot sun without sighting prey," he said. "But when the crew did spot a whale or a large fish, they were galvanized into action. It all reminded me of Herman Melville's descriptions of whaling in *Moby Dick*."

Melville recalled the whales of the waters of the Lesser Sundas in his immortal work: "Was it not so, O Timor Tom! thou famed Leviathan scarred like an iceberg, who so long did'st lurk in the oriental straits of that name, whose spout was oft seen from the palmy beach of Ombay?"

Vessels like the *Pusaka* are called *peledang* and are sturdily handcrafted for the strenuous hunts from several kinds of wood. The curved hulls are bound with rattan or pegged. Joints are caulked with natural tar, then rubbed or "fed" as the locals would say, with manta ray brains and chicken blood to seal in the boat's spiritual essence. Despite inroads made by Catholicism, Lembata islanders still cling to many old beliefs.

The *peledang* measure 10 to 12-meters long and two-meters wide at the beam. They are lashed with outriggers on each side for stability. Large pieces of wood used in construction are positioned the way the tree grew with trunks rooted to the deck to maintain the cosmic forces of life. And eyes are painted on the prow to enable the boat to "see" should the helmsman fail at his task.

The *molang*, a shaman, sprinkles new boats with chicken blood to infuse them with life. The boats of the whalers of Lembata are treated as living entities. The passage of life into the *peledang*, unlike the taking of a life of a whale, is a sacred moment. In contrast to modern-day whalers, under constant criticism from environmental groups, Lembata's men respect their prey enough to do battle without the use of 20th century weaponry. They confront the whale on its own terms — at the risk of sustaining serious injuries or even losing their lives.

Despite their primitive techniques, the men of Lembata catch an average of about 30 whales a year. They do not ravage the whale population like the well-armed whaling fleets of other countries. Manta rays and sharks are also harpooned, but sperm whales are the most lucrative catch. Other whales are fair game in years when food is scarce. Few crops grow in Lamalera and the villagers barter whale and fish meat with inland peoples for rice and corn. Two kilograms of manta ray meat buys 100 ears of corn and five medium-sized strips of shark meat can fetch 20 kilograms of rice. It is forbidden to hunt the blue whale, the totemic symbol of one clan.

In earlier years, the crews commenced the whaling season with the ritual polishing and anointing of ancestral skulls, a throwback to the pre-Catholic days of cannibalism and head-hunting. The skulls were worshiped and enshrined at the back of each

The late Raja of Melolo, a village on the northeast coast of Sumba, models an exquisite *hinggi* wrap from his royal collection of *ikat*. The finest *ikat* is worn during important ceremonies and rituals. Note that the ivory handle of a traditional kris dagger pokes out from one corner of the Raja's regal wrap.

A crew member of a whaling *peledang* (above) lunges at a whale shark with harpoon. Jubilant whalers and villagers haul a sperm whale ashore (right) on Lembata and butcher it for food. By tradition, a share of each catch is given to the descendants of the indigenous inhabitants of the village of Lamalera.

clan's boat shed. In modern times, a Catholic priest blesses the armada before it sets out in early May.

"The *Pusaka* had been launched in 1968 and had caught more than 30 whales by the time I was allowed to join the crew," Kal said. "Before setting sail each morning, one man pulled off a plaited leaf cover from the painted eyes on its prow. That made sure the boat would see its way past the island's treacherous coral reefs without any incident.

"I joined the men in prayer then grabbed an oar and, to the rhythm of a song, helped paddle out to sea. A handful of other boats set out simultaneously, gliding smoothly across the calm waters. The men raised two tall bamboo spars that had been lashed together at the top and one corner of the plaited rectangular sail pulled to the top enabled the vessel to jibe easily or sail close to the wind.

"Each man had a specific task; there were lookouts, sail handlers, a steersman, bailer, harpooner and assistant. The harpooner began sharpening his spearhead after the sail had been hoisted. The heads were forged from chunks of old automobile chassis and a hunk of whetstone was used to hone each cutting edge. A long coil of resin-coated handspun cotton rope attached to the harpoon ensured that a securely-hooked whale would not get away even if it towed the boat for several days, as

occasionally happened. Several fishing lines were also put out; light ones for flying fish and a thicker one for bigger fish. Then part of the crew drifted off to sleep, while the rest kept watch on the waters.

"I had a designated space on the *Pusaka*, out of the way astern on my own little coil of rope. The spot next to me was occupied by Antonius, an ex-chief of the village. When we weren't napping, Antonius asked the kinds of questions I had been asked so many times before in other parts of Indonesia: How much did it cost to come to Indonesia from America? How long did it take to get to Lembata? How much money did people earn in my country? How many men had gone to the moon? Had I gone to the moon yet?

"Antonius told me that the ancestors of the people of Lamalera came from Sulawesi, the big island to the north once called Celebes. During a migration that lasted more than 200 years, they traveled in a wide arc, often spending a generation or more on Ceram or Ambon before settling on Lembata. Mostly fishermen, they negotiated with the indigenous people of the island for the privilege of staying. Thus, when a whale or large fish is caught, a share must always be set aside for the clan which lived in Lamalera before the fishermen got there.

"My conversations with Antonius enlivened the

long, dull days of cruising and waiting. We usually returned with the shore breeze in mid-afternoon. The day's catch was divided among the crew. The harpooner would pop out the eyes of the small fish and eat them raw, a culinary habit he believed would help him see better.

"We drifted for days without sighting any large fish, let alone whales, and I was beginning to think I had jinxed the boat. Then one morning just as we started rowing, a whale shark surfaced no more than 10 meters off the starboard bow. The harpooner hastily slammed a metal head onto its shaft, then jumped on his prey like a rodeo cowboy mounting a bucking bronco. He managed to open a gash in the shark, but the harpoon head had not yet been sharpened that day and it didn't hold.

"Missing the easy prey depressed the crew, but spirits soared again about an hour later when another large fish appeared nearby. It was a marlin. Indonesians call them *ikan raja*, the 'king of fish.' This time the men were prepared; nerves taut, muscles straining. Antonius grunted as we rowed with all our strength and willpower. The harpooner poised on the prow launched his spear with deadly accuracy, then followed it overboard.

"Even as the harpooner was scrambling back aboard, the marlin had managed to take out more than 50 meters of line in its struggle to jerk the spear out. Three lengths of rope had to be tied together and let out before the marlin began to weaken. Slowly the men began to pull in their catch, only to give back a few meters when the marlin panicked and managed to find a hidden reserve of energy. More than a half-hour passed before the fish surfaced again. It made the mistake of coming up near the boat. The vigilant harpooner immediately finished off the marlin with another expertly-aimed thrust of his weapon. After the long weeks of bad luck, the faces of the crew lit up jubilantly.

"No sooner had everyone relaxed than another whale shark cruised past. And we were off on a 'Sunda sleighride' again. One plunge of a harpoon was enough. The fish gave up without a struggle.

"'Too stupid to fight,' Antonius said. He explained that the Indonesian name for the whale shark was *ikan iuh bodoh*, literally 'dumb fish.'

"*Ikan iuh bodoh* was too large to haul aboard ship so the men butchered it in the water. They pushed large chunks of meat over the gunwhales. I tried to tell them the bloodied sea might attract dangerous sharks. But they just laughed. 'We hope so. Then we can harpoon them too.'

"With our big catch on board, we headed for shore where the traditional exchange took place. The crew got several bamboo tubes of *tuak*, fermented palm wine, in exchange for a portion of fish.

"On the way back to Lamalera, we ate pieces of raw marlin and washed them down with the *tuak*. The spirits fueled the men's exuberant mood. When we beached the boat, dozens of children scrambled aboard. They eagerly helped push the *Pusaka* back to its shed in hopes of a free handout. Then the fish was sliced into manageable portions and divided among the crew, the boat builder and the 'landowners.' Even I received a share, not as much as crew members with families to feed. But my several kilos of prime meat were more than symbolic.

"A little later, another boat returned from sea with a large sperm whale. It had been a lucky day for the whalers of Lembata. The whale was so large the villagers spent the entire next day butchering it. That day at sea provided plenty of meat with which to barter for rice and corn and other staples. When I sailed away the next day, I was satiated. The happiness of the villagers filled me with a sense of well-being."

Although most people of Flores are Catholics, there remains a strong undercurrent of ancient beliefs like those of the sullen-faced high priest in the colorful headdress (above). Ancestral beliefs remain strong on Sumba where the size and number of water buffalo horns is indicative of the wealth and powers of the man (right) who was believed by neighbors to be a sorcerer.

Chapter Seven

In the Land of Dayaks and Bugis

Wherein our intrepid Narrator, having neglected to rub Earth into his Navel to ward off Evil, survives a bloody Encounter in the Rain Forests of Borneo while our Photographer sets out on a Quest for Headhunters; on the island of Sulawesi, the Pair makes a startling Discovery in the Caves of Torajaland and explores the enchanted seas of Bunaken.

Some Indonesians take unusual precautions when visiting Borneo. "My grandfather told me when you go to Kalimantan, when you step off the plane or boat, you must do so with the right foot, then reach down and scoop up a handful of earth and rub it in your navel before putting your left foot on the ground. Then you must pray *Bismillah'irahmani'r–rahim,* 'In the name of Allah, the merciful, the charitable.' Only then can you be sure to return safely, my friend."

For Kal and I, the sage advice was a bit late. It came from Agus, an aide in the tourist department in Ujung Pandang. Though unaware of the prescribed precaution of rubbing dirt in our bellybuttons, we both survived several visits to Indonesian Borneo.

Still, it never hurts to follow advice when traveling in Indonesia, especially if it comes from as sagacious a source as a grandfather and especially when poking around in places like Kalimantan. In all of Indonesia it is Kalimantan, the Indonesian two-thirds of the island of Borneo, that lives up to its reputation. It is an exotic, equatorial island in every sense of the words: a damp blanket of smothering tropical jungles creased with twisting rivers, a forbidding domain wild with giant trees choked by vines, alive with orangutans and 10-meter long pythons, swarming with horrendous insects that grow to outrageous sizes, where headhunters once stalked game and their fellow humans with poison darts spat from hollowed-out bamboo blowpipes.

I got my first taste of Kalimantan when I wrote a story on the reforestation efforts of American timber companies that were felling trees in large concessions. The companies operate out of big camps along the Mahakam River, a busy commercial and transportation thoroughfare that winds for 700 kilometers right into the heart of the island.

The Fokker Friendship nosed out of a sea of clouds into Sepinggan Airport. Because it serves the enormous oil and gas industry in the area, Sepinggan is the busiest airport in the country next to Jakarta's, in spite of a runway that is so short pilots have to take off almost vertically leaving passengers with their hearts in their mouths. A wood-paneled jalopy of indeterminate manufacture took me into Balikpapan, East Kalimantan's bustling but nondescript provincial capital. The city was noted only for an American-style suburb on a hillside constructed by the state's Pertamina Oil Company and known to the locals as Beverly Hills. A few hours later I was in Samarinda on a boat heading up the mouth of the Mahakam, a yawning, muddy four-kilometer gap jammed with waterborne vessels. There were also log jams, real ones not the proverbial kind. Logs that seemed to be the size of California redwoods, some lashed together to form rafts, bobbed in the murky river water distressingly close to our craft. As the hours passed and we left Samarinda far behind in our wake, the boat floated through patches of secondary forest. The air was filled with birds and I caught glimpses of several hornbills, a symbol of fertility in Kalimantan and other parts of Indonesia.

I spent several days upriver at the Weyerhaeuser timber camp, a simple but comfortable enclave of prefabricated cabins equipped with modern appliances powered by generators, an oasis of hospitality swamped by the inhospitable Borneo jungle. I relaxed by watching a video in the recreation room.

Darkness had swallowed the jungle by the time I attempted to walk down a lighted corridor to my guest cabin. But the passage was swarming with flying, buzzing insects, the size of which I had never

Intrigue lies around every bend of the mighty rivers of Indonesian Borneo. Revelers at the Erau festival held in Tenggarong in East Kalimantan lower a long "dragon" into the muddy Mahakam (preceding pages) where its wooden head was ritually severed and its rattan skeleton allowed to float away. At right, a Dayak man tops a totem with a headband of the national colors.

imagined, hordes of them attracted by the fluorescent bulbs. I carefully stepped into the corridor, my arms covering my head, but backed off when the monsters began dive bombing me. I took my chances with a dark, unilluminated path instead, at a quickstep. At the door of my cabin, I long-jumped past another pair of lightbulbs that had attracted squadrons of winged bugs, slamming the door behind me before chancing the lightswitch. A cockroach as big as a mouse ducked into the bathroom. I turned in and slept.

I did not lose any blood to jungle denizens until the next day, however. Up at the crack of dawn to what sounded like the entire bird and insect population of the earth announcing the new day in ear-shattering unison, I traveled by boat and Land Rover to a logging operation. John, an American, was the guide. At one point, a family of agitated gibbons glared at us after we disturbed their snooze on the road. John rolled up his window. The apes looked like they were in an aggressive mood, stretching their arms and baring their teeth.

We drove over a new rugged dirt road to a spot in the thickening jungle where men and machines were doggedly and noisily wrestling to bring down meranti (*shorea* in Latin) trees and other versions of Borneo's 400 species of dipterocarps. Soaring up to 70 meters, these giant hardwoods make excellent lumber because they have straight trunks that are bare of side branches below 35 meters, John explained. He stopped in at his prefabricated office and I followed him through the door, startled to find the walls inside coated with an astonishing number of moths and butterflies as big as fruit bats with wings painted in perfect patterns of impossible colors. The insects seemed to be pinned up as decorations. I complimented John on his butterfly collection. He turned to me and laughed. "Look again, it's not a collection.

I put out a finger to touch one of the moths. It flew away. "That was Raja Brooke's birdwing," John said. "Also known as *Troides brookiana*."

The "specimens" on the wall were live insects that had simply parked there for a rest. John said that when he first began working there he tried shooing away his wall coverings in the mornings, getting to know the species in the process, but they always returned the next day. Now he didn't bother. In

Indonesia's ubiquitous Bugis schooners with their tall wooden masts and wide beamed hulls dwarf a group of merchants in small wooden canoes on the Barito River. The schooners grace the wharves of Banjarmasin, the provincial capital of South Kalimantan built on the river. The Barito flows 650 kilometers through Borneo's interior.

fact, he hardly noticed them anymore until visitors came in and made remarks as silly as mine.

My next encounter with Borneo jungle life occurred near camp, in a virgin stand of trees that had been labeled for the benefit of visitors. It looked like an easy walk yet everyone was wearing ankle high boots and carrying a *parang*, Indonesia's handy machete. I followed, unarmed and in tennis shoes.

The variety and magnitude of the trees was captivating. Their leafy tops were almost invisible from the ground where lianas and epiphytes and other parasitic vines dangled. We saw the Pitcher Plant, a carnivore which munches on insects that unsuspectingly trigger the trap door on its yellow-spotted auburn pod. As we walked deeper into the jungle, the damp path seemed to be in motion. I looked closer. We were walking over layers of long, thin worms that wriggled and leaped at my shoes. "Leeches," was all someone said, "Yuchh," was all I could think as my feet cringed in my tennis shoes.

If there was one abomination that I would rather not have encountered in life, it was *Haemadipsa zeylanica*, Borneo's infamous ground leech. As he and his relatives undulated up my ankles in search of a juicy vein, I had the urge to sprint back to the jeep. But there was my pride to think about. Everyone else in the party was merely scraping off the repugnant creatures with their *parang*.

"Here," said one of the Indonesians, who was aware of my discomfort as he watched me trying to tiptoe through the leeches, and handed me his weapon. I valiantly tried to halt the charging annelids, using the blade to peel them off my ankles, all of them, I thought. When we emerged from the jungle, a guide suggested I take off my shoes and socks. I did. They were soaked with blood. Several leeches, swollen fat with blood, had embedded their suckers in the soles of my feet. They had wormed their way right through my socks!

Borneo is an island big enough to engulf all of the British Isles and then some, bigger than France or Texas. It is virtually bisected by the equator. The southern two-thirds was part of the Dutch East Indies and was incorporated into Indonesia after independence. Northern Borneo, former British colonies conquered in the 19th century by a swashbuckling "White Raja," James Brooke, the

The network of rivers that flows through Borneo's jungles are the only transportation
link between some of the island's villages. They also provide a source of nourishment and
an occupation for this man who earns his keep by weaving nets for the local fishermen.
The craftsman takes special pains to impart the right weave to his handicraft.

man who gave his name to one of the island's species of butterflies, has now been parceled into the East Malaysian states of Sarawak and Sabah and independent Brunei Darussalam, a sultanate rich in oil.

The Indonesians have subdivided their part of the island into four provinces, all told containing no more than seven million people. That makes Kalimantan one of the world's least-peopled land masses. Residents that have migrated from elsewhere, like the Bugis and Javanese, congregate around the major cities especially Banjarmasin on the mouth of the Barito River in South Kalimantan, and Pontianak, the seat of West Kalimantan which also has a large percentage of Chinese, and Balikpapan. The indigenous population of about 1.5 million is composed of tribes collectively called Dayaks who live in villages in the jungle far up the meandering rivers of Borneo.

The word Kalimantan may have been derived from Kali, (there are always dissenting opinions), the Malay word for river. The major rivers are the Barito, at 650 kilometers, which flows through the south; the Mahakam in the east; and the 1,150-kilometer Kapuas, the island's longest, in the west. They merge with the sea at wide estuaries that were river valleys before they were inundated by the global rise in the sea level after the Ice Age. Laden with silt, the rivers have deposited sediment forming vast swamps in the lowlands from Pontianak to Banjarmasin. Rivers and their tributaries are Kalimantan's primary transportation networks. Calm and navigable for long stretches, they become torrents of white rapids and whirlpools in places, especially after the sudden gales of rain that are a feature of the island's weather patterns.

In addition to its mighty rivers, Kalimantan is sprinkled with lowland lakes. There are at least 110 in the interior, including the Jempang (15,000 hectares), Semayang (13,000 hectares), and Melintang (11,000 hectares). Compared to other islands of Indonesia, Kalimantan is rather flat except for several disconnected mountain ranges in the central and eastern hinterlands which are the source of its rivers. Gunung Raya in the Schwaner Range, rising to 2,278 meters, is Kalimantan's highest mountain and the second highest on the island after Mt. Kinabalu (4,101 meters) in Sabah. Compared to other parts of Indonesia, Kalimantan is also geologi-

cally peaceful. There are no active volcanos, one of the reasons for the island's poor soil.

Still, the unyielding Borneo jungle has so far resisted modern development, even road construction. In fact, it took 16 Land Rovers (well-equipped with picks, machetes and radios, and drivers schooled in bridge-building techniques and wilderness survival), 12 days just to traverse 1,600 kilometers of Kalimantan from Balikpapan to Kota Bangun during the 1985 running of the Camel Trophy Off-Road Rally — and they had to be airlifted part of the way by helicopters. A British writer who rode in the convoy wrote that "danger was a constant companion on the narrow track hacked through Borneo's dense, sweltering jungle … a nightmare of deep gullies, knee-high mud, fallen trees and the ever-present threat of landslides triggered by the fury of torrential tropical rains."

East Kalimantan and its Mahakam River have been important throughout Borneo's history as the seat of the archipelago's earliest civilization, Kutai. Inscriptions on seven stone sacrificial poles, called *yupas*, discovered near Muara Kaman along the Mahakam are even older than the engravings on the *Prasasti Tugu* found near Jakarta. They indicate that a Hindu kingdom was already thriving in East Kalimantan by the fifth century A.D. The inscriptions are attributed to a King Mulawarman, founder of a line of kings which evolved into the Kutai Dynasty. According to local folklore, Mulawarman was one of the twin sons of King Rama and Sita, the star-crossed lovers and heros of the *Ramayana* epic. Mulawarman's Hindu empire came to be known as Kutai Kertanegara. Indonesian chronicler Nenny Wirakusumah credits the Chinese with some of the terminology of the area. She wrote:

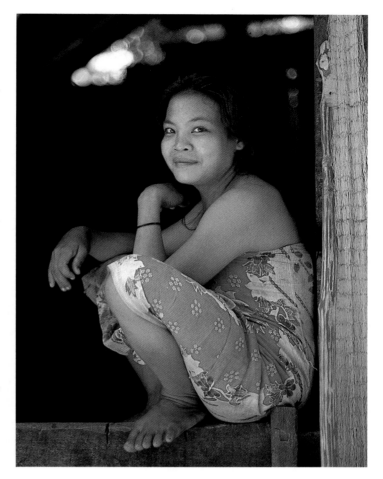

> "When the Chinese first came to the area and observed the 'big river' they exclaimed 'Maha Kam' — and since then the river has been named Mahakam; and after they learned how large the land was, they said 'Ko Tai' which means 'great country,' and Kutai it has been ever since."

Kutai's rulers converted to Islam in the 16th century with the coming of Arab merchants. Dynastic changes brought about the shifting of Kutai's power base downstream from Muara Kaman at

A contented baby gently bounces to dreamland in an ingenious hammock (left) that his mother rigged up from a sarong while cruising on the Mahakam aboard a water taxi. As one travels upriver in Kalimantan, pretty smiles are common (above).

A fisherman in a dugout canoe floats in front of a village mosque as he prepares his nets for a day's work on tranquil Lake Jempang (above). In another part of East Kalimantan the busy Mahakam River is the scene of massive logging activities (following pages). Enormous logs are lashed together and floated to sawmills downstream.

Tenggarong in 1782. The last of the line of Kutai kings, Aji Sultan Muhammad Parikesit, died at the palace in Tenggarong in 1960. But the kings' power had been effectively curtailed since the Dutch took over the area in 1844.

The country's lucrative oil industry got its start in East Kalimantan at the turn-of-the-century when British Petroleum discovered wells in Balikpapan and on the offshore island of Tarakan. Today, jumbles of steel and iron stacks and conduits of oil and gas works protrude from Tarakan and the seas around it like immense abstract metal sculptures. It is because of petroleum and its by-products and timber that East Kalimantan accounted for 25 per cent of Indonesia's total export earnings in an average year in the 1970s and early 1980s.

Logging is concentrated in the vast forests west of Balikpapan and Samarinda. Sadly, this very area was the scene of what the Paris-based International Union for the Conservation of Nature has called the greatest environmental disaster of the century and possibly in recorded history. A fire, apparently started by a combination of slash-and-burn cultivation and a long drought that had turned the moist forest floor into combustible tinder, blazed from late 1982 until the middle of 1983. The flames consumed more than 3.5-million hectares of economically-invaluable and ecologically-fragile woodlands, an area greater than that of Netherlands. The government estimated that about U.S.$6 billion in timber was lost. Even more disturbing, experts doubt whether the damage of the delicate jungle ecosystem will ever repair itself.

Life in South Kalimantan revolves around Banjarmasin, a city on stilts, laced with canals, bustling with floating markets and speedy "water taxis." Diamond mining and cutting still goes on at Cempaka, about 40 kilometers from Banjarmasin. The diamonds and semi-precious stones, coal and copper attracted Dutch traders to this old sultanate as long ago as the 16th century, but gems have ceased to be economically important.

Palangka Raya in Central Kalimantan is a relatively new city, established in 1957, and the site of a 35-kilometer road to nowhere built with Russian aid during the Sukarno era. Many of the Dayaks from the interior travel to markets in Palangka Raya by boat. An orangutan research and rehabilitation

center is located in Central Kalimantan's 300,000-hectare Tanjung Puting Preserve.

With 2.5-million people, West Kalimantan is the most populous province. Rubber plantations along the Kapuas River are the best in Indonesia outside of Sumatra. The provincial capital, Pontianak, is Kalimantan's biggest city and is located at 0 degrees north 0 degrees south latitude, smack on the equator.

Borneo. **The name has stayed** with me since childhood when I had seen a television program in which a circus attraction billed as "The Wild Man of Borneo" featured prominently. The so-called "Wild Man" was, of course, Hollywood's version of the indigenous people known as Dayaks.

Far from being the crude and primitive savages depicted by Hollywood, the Dayaks have a sophisticated culture. They are skilled boatmen and hunters and experts at living in the hostile jungles. They are craftsmen who make exquisite *ikat* weaving and unique wooden carvings and totems. They use glass beads and bird plumes to turn their ceremonial costumes into complementary explosions of color and design. They once transformed their own bodies into works of art with superbly wrought tattoos that sometimes covered them from their heads to the tips of their fingers and toes, but the practice, like so many customs, is fading.

Traditionally, the Dayaks' highly-organized social system revolves around the longhouse, another facet of life that is disappearing. Some of these wooden habitations on pilings are up to 150 meters in length and 15 meters wide. The largest have 200 doors and house 100 families. One of its narrow doors customarily faces east where the life-giving sun rises and windows are sometimes stuffed with grass to prevent malevolent spirits from getting in at night. Each family has its own compartment for privacy, but much of daily life is communal and takes place in the enclosed, unpartitioned corridor that runs the length of the longhouse. Baskets, blowpipes, paddles and other household utensils are stored on planks above the corridor. Some of the tribes carve dragons, snakes and birds into their architecture and these serve as both splendid decoration and protection against evil spirits. In recent decades, however, the longhouses have been vanishing, replaced by contemporary blockhouse dwellings housing one or two families. Tradition is giving way to comfort.

With the disappearance of the longhouses has gone some of the old Dayak customs. Distended earlobes weighed down with heavy rings, once a sign of beauty, are rarely seen among younger Dayak women now. But the men are remaining mum on the subject of the *palang*, a crossbar of bone inserted in the end of the penis, patterned on the natural *palang* of the Borneo rhinoceros, that is designed to provide added sexual pleasure for women. Those young men asked whether the *palang* is still popular just grinned and declined comment.

"Dayak" is a catch-all name for about 200 individual groups, each with its own language and customs. Most prevalent are the Iban, Kayan and Kenyah. The nomadic Punan are considered to have had the least contact with the 20th century. Some of the old Punan people still have tattoos and wear wooden ear pegs and the Prince Valiant haircuts that resemble those of the early Beatles. Reputed to be great hunters, many have hung up their blowpipes for axes and hoes and become farmers.

Kal went in search of "*asli*" Dayaks in East Kalimantan when he boarded a regular river taxi called *Air Bungga*, "Flower Water," and endured three days cramped into "one-and-a-half meters of vertical space" on the Mahakam. Bathroom procedures proved to be a serious problem on the ride. The toilet was a hole in a platform that hung above the rushing water in the stern, "enclosed" for modesty's sake by knee-high planks. Kal attracted the rapt attention of the other passengers who were all Indonesians whenever he tried to maneuver himself into a squat over the toilet and, unable to function in front of an audience, resigned himself to constipation for most of the trip.

Air Bungga took Kal to a tributary of the Mahakam, the Kedang Kepala, "severed head", and a settlement of Kenyahs called Slabing. From there, he squeezed himself and his equipment into a wobbly dugout with a sputtering motor in which he pushed three hours further upriver to its last outpost, Ben Hes, a village of 71 families. There, after chatting with the headman, Burham Mas, in his stilt house, Kal was invited to stay with the headman and his family as long as he wished.

Burham Mas was a descendant of the rajas of the region who had a high school education but

A striking ornament of colored beads and leopard's teeth and a belt of coins (top left), heavy brass earrings and a headband of beads and feathers (top right), and brightly-embroidered and beaded sarongs (bottom right) and a baby backpack (bottom left) are hallmarks of the artistic heritage of Borneo's Dayaks.

During tribal rituals in East Kalimantan, Dayak men dance in a frenzy around a water buffalo that is about to be sacrificed to ancestral spirits (top) while a bevy of suitably impressed young ladies look on (bottom). The buffalo bleeds to death (right) after its neck has been slit according to religious custom.

nonetheless worked the fields alongside his people. Although a recent convert to Catholicism, he still adhered to some of the ways of his ancestors. Fortunately, head-hunting was not one of them.

Head-hunting and cannibalism were an integral part of the rites associated with animist beliefs of groups in many of the islands of the Indonesian archipelago, but Borneo has been synonymous with head-hunting, probably as a result of hair-raising tales told by colonial era British soldiers-of-fortune ruminating over gin slings at the Raffles Hotel Long Bar in Singapore. Burham Mas said that in the old days his people believed that freshly-severed heads insured the welfare of a village. He also said that all Dayak groups believed the head to be the source of the most powerful forms of magic. The capture of an enemy's head transferred the defeated man's spiritual energies to the warrior who had taken it as well as to his village. Important chieftains demanded three or four freshly-severed heads as payment for the promise of their daughters in marriage. If proper attention was lavished on the skulls, if they received offerings of food and tobacco, Dayaks believed they would protect the village from disease, bring rain and a big crop. New skulls were required at all the great events of a village life — the building of longhouses, marriage or funerary rituals, the unveiling of an important carving and, in the endless circle of combat, power in wars waged to obtain more skulls.

Like anything else, the magic of old heads ebbed with age so the men of the tribe regularly donned their war gear, whipped out their blowpipes and went in search of new battles, a practice that led to a virtual permanent state of tribal warfare in the Borneo hinterlands. The British and the Dutch managed to end most head-hunting and tribal warfare. The last confirmed cases were the handiwork of Iban allies of the British during Sukarno's military confrontation over Malaysia's claim to North Borneo in the early 1960s. But, as can be expected in such mysterious regions, there is talk that head-hunting still occurs on occasion in the interior. In 1985, Jakarta's *Sinar Harapan* newspaper reported that the government had charged four men in Central Kalimantan with beheading two timber company workers and eating some of their liver and flesh following ancient ritual practices.

Kenyah Dayaks from a remote village of Borneo where head-hunting was once an important tradition, sit proudly round a prized trophy as if they had just returned from a successful raid. As part of the reenactment of the ancient custom, the skull of an orangutan was used as a substitute for that of a freshly-severed human head.

The ancestor who was divine
The forefather revered as a lord
Built that which has a roof high-pitched,
Set up that which on tall poles stands,
The bua *feast stone set in place*
The ritual bamboo planted.

   – from the Sa'adan Toraja Chant for the Deceased

The Bugis people who inhabit many Indonesian islands and are highly visible in the coastal cities and villages of Kalimantan, hail from the large island east of Borneo known to history as Celebes, but now called Sulawesi. Its most famous city and home port of the seafaring Bugis was formerly called Makassar, but the Indonesians, seeking to erase unpleasant memories of the colonial past, have changed its name to Ujung Pandang which means "point of sight".

Sulawesi's odd shape gives the island more than its share of coastline. Australian journalist Maslyn Williams wrote that the island resembles a "limp starfish." Its arms are four lanky peninsulas joined by a mountainous midsection. The southern extremities are pimpled with limestone nodules and swollen with the furrowed, yet fertile highlands of burned out volcanos. The contours of the north are more soft and rounded and volcanos there still erupt.

Approximately ten million people live on the island. In addition to the Bugis and Makassarese, whose chief difference appears to be linguistic, Sulawesi's ethnic composition includes the Torajans, Minahasans and smaller groups like the Seku, Loinang, Muna and Balantak and the Konjo people of Tanah Towa. Lying east of the Wallace Line, Sulawesi is another of the transition zones between the flora and fauna of Asia and Australia.

Of the island's four provinces, South Sulawesi is the most populous. A little more than six million live in its 85,000 square kilometers, two-thirds of them Bugis. Comprising the southwestern arm of the "star," South Sulawesi is splashed by the Straits of Makassar along its 700-kilometer long west coast, the Flores Sea in the south where the province narrows to a 100 kilometer wide isthmus and, the Bay of Bone (pronounced "bow-nay") that curves for more than 500 kilometers along its eastern coast and separates it from the sister province of Southeast Sulawesi. It is a protean world of dry, windswept salt flats, rain forests and precipitous limestone cliffs hewn in the earth by prehistoric tidal action. The island's highest peak, 3,455-meter high Rantekombola, rises at the northern end of the province.

Anthropologists believe parts of South Sulawesi, like Central Java, may have been inhabited by ancestors of modern man. Primitive stone tools found in the area have been carbon-dated back to a half million years ago. Later migrations of people came from South and Southeast Asia, including India and the Philippines. Red fingerprints and painted scrawls discovered in caves near the town of Maros, about 40 kilometers north of Ujung Pandang, are believed to be the handiwork of people who lived there some 5,000 to 10,000 years ago.

By the time the Portuguese came looking for spices in the 16th century, a number of elites had emerged. The dominant kingdoms were the Luwu in the north, Bone in the eastern part of the modern province and Gowa based in Makassar. Despite long trading contacts with other Muslim ports in Indonesia, it was not until the end of the 16th century that the sultans of Gowa and its Bugis and Makassarese subjects adopted Islam. Today, the people of the area are among the most fervent, fundamentalist Muslims in the archipelago.

Utilizing the seafaring skills and daring of its Bugis subjects, Gowa brought large parts of East Kalimantan, the Lesser Sundas, the central and southern Moluccas islands, the Riau Archipelago and even Temasek under its influence. Temasek later became Singapore, the island city that borrowed the name Bugis for the main street in its most infamous, now-defunct, nightlife district. The Bugis of Gowa traded with China, Burma, India and the Philippines. They even traveled as far south as Australia in search of sea cucumbers which they used for barter with merchants of the Chinese empire.

The Portuguese cultivated a working relationship with Gowa and built a fortress on Makassar's strategic and excellent harbor. But it was the Dutch who forcibly wrested control of the city in 1667 and made it a key link in international trade routes. Hall called it a "halfway house between Java and the Spice Islands" in his *History of Southeast Asia*. The Bugis resented Dutch interference and resisted it. They later fought valiantly for independence.

One of the most impressive sights in all of Indonesia today is the magnficent *pinisi* schooner built by the Bugis much the same way they have constructed it for centuries. We saw the skeletons of new ships under construction on a golden beach in Biru on the southeastern shores of South Sulawesi. The carpenters there said it takes 15 men an entire year to complete one of the wooden-hulled giants. The schooners are launched with great fanfare as up to a thousand men push the ships out to sea.

Tongkanan **roofs shaped like boat hulls** and headgear shaped like water buffalo horns (preceding pages) are common symbols of South Sulawesi's Torajan culture. Uncommon is the beauty of Bugis women like this young lady of Sengkang (right).

"Would you kindly kick that skull** out of the way for me?" Kal asked me as he fiddled with his Nikons. "Never mind, I'll do it myself." Kal nudged the human skull with the toe of his shoe and it went clattering down the slope, over piles of tibias, femurs and other assorted human bones that cluttered the ground. After several days clambering up cliffs and nosing into caves littered with skeletons and sarcophagi made from tree trunks, their contents often spilling out, we were not the least bit fazed by the macabre tableaux of Torajaland.

For centuries, the people of Torajaland in South Sulawesi's cool, scenic highlands, have interred their deceased relatives in natural caves and hand-carved niches in the sheer limestone escarpments that are a prominent part of their landscape. The eerie air of some of these grisly burial grounds is enhanced by rows of lifelike wooden effigies. Entire families of these figures stare out from "balconies" in the limestone facades at Lemo and Londa, "keeping watch" over the graves and the adjoining *padi* fields, lasting reminders to the Torajans of the presence of the spirits of their ancestors. Offerings of bottles filled with water and flower petals placed on rocks near the effigies are evidence that the unique religion, *Aluk Todolo*, still exerts strong influence, even though the majority of the Torajans have been converted by Protestant missionaries.

Aluk Todolo in the Torajan language means "rituals of the ancestors." At its core is the belief that the souls of the ancestors control the lives of their descendants. The complex rituals that Torajaland is noted for are all designed to keep the ancestors happy so that they in turn will make life pleasant for their earthbound relatives. The religion acknowledges the existence of a Supreme Being, Pong Matua, who reigns over a team of gods.

Every aspect of life, even the striking architecture of traditional Torajan homes, is associated with *Aluk Todolo*. The original builder of the home, or *tongkonan*, with its sweeping roof, is revered by descendants as the family founder. Thus, the *tongkonan* becomes the focal point of the family as it passes down from generation to generation. One school of thought holds that the design of the arched rooftops is patterned on the shape of the grand sailing vessels in which the forefathers of the Torajans migrated to Sulawesi. They were proto-Malays who are believed to have come from Indochina around 2,500 B.C. This theory would also help to explain the shipbuilding skills of the Bugis. The facades of the *tongkonan* are always erected pointing north (facing the realm of the gods), so the gods can enter through the front door. Exteriors are decorated

with designs of plants, animals and geometric patterns meticulously painted with black, white, yellow and red colors extracted from natural substances. Buffalo horns adorn some *tongkonan*, their number and size indicative of the family's social rank. Traditional Torajan society functioned along class lines.

The ubiquitous water buffalo is prized in Toraja-land not only as meat and as the workhorse that pulls the plows through the rice fields, but as the highest form of offering to the gods and ancestors. Kal and I visited the water buffalo and pig market in Rantepao, a picturesque village on the Saqdan River that caters to tourists. A scaled-down *tongkonan* is the centerpiece of the town square. At the market hundreds of pigs, hoofs bound and lashed to bamboo carrying poles, grunt and squeal as owners buy and swap. We were told that the most sacred buffalos were the albinos with big humps and pink spots. They command prices of up to two million rupiah, roughly the equivalent of U.S. $2,000. The pigs, some of them the size of baby rhinos, were laid in bondage in long rows in a pavilion as shoppers inspected them. Whenever one of the discriminating buyers jabbed one of the slobbering creatures in the ribs, it would snort and jerk – and every other pig in the place followed suit as if they were all hooked to the same central nervous system.

Word was out that preparations for an *Aluk Tomate*, the ritual for the dead, were underway in the rocky hills outside town. Naturally, the location was at the end of another rutted, spine-shattering road, past a graveyard where some mausoleums were topped by *tongkonan*, the traditional "vehicles" for transporting souls to heaven. One grave was topped with a stone carving of an airplane.

When we arrived, hundreds of people were already gathered in a steep-sided valley about a 20-minute, up-and-down walk on wooded mountain paths from the main road. Water buffalos were being tethered to trees and stakes on the slope. Live pigs bound in bamboo were being heaped in piles on the grounds like cordwood. The *tongkonan* had been plastered with red banners and wrapping paper for the occasion, and on one tall platform on a pair of stilts under a *tongkonan* roof, the place of honor, were two tubular coffins painted in red with gold stars and crucifixes. Newly-built viewing enclosures encircled the ceremonial grounds and housed the hundreds of guests who had been invited. I counted 82 cubicles in all, each neatly numbered. We arrived with gifts of *kretek* cigarettes and bags of rice which we presented to a man wearing a *peci*, sarong and black shirt who was apparently in charge of the festivities. His name was Johannes Rahantepasan.

A row of eerie wooden effigies "sit" on a balcony erected on the limestone facade of a Torajan burial cave (left) at Londa. Inside the cave, human skulls and skeletons (above) spill out from coffins that are painted with symbols of new and old religions.

Torajan women keep vigil for a deceased relative whose remains are wrapped in red-and-gold and rest on an elaborate catafalque. The women have prepared dishes of raw vegetables for the hundreds of guests attending the large funeral in South Sulawesi's highlands. *Aluk Tomate*, the Torajan ritual for the dead, is a festive affair.

He introduced us to a loquacious middle-aged woman named Adriana who said she was a Catholic, but confessed that she still followed some of the ancient *adat* of Torajaland. "The family wants the funeral that way, so that's the way it must be," she said.

Judging by the rapidly multiplying number of water buffalos and pigs and guests, we had obviously stumbled upon the funeral for the departed souls of a well-off, high-caste family. According to Stanislaus Sandarupa, a young expert on his culture, the Torajans view death as the pinnacle of life, the freeing of the spirit from earthly bonds that enables it to go to *puya*, the land of souls. Until the ceremonies are held, the deceased is thought of as incurably ill rather than dead or, in the local language, "lying waving like an eel." Only after the ritual is the soul released for the trip to paradise.

Celebrations can involve up to a week of dancing, sport, and feasting, depending on the caste of the deceased. Relatives wear black mourning clothes, abstain from eating rice and drop a cat from a high place as a symbolic suicide to emphasize the family's sorrow that they will never meet their loved one again in the temporal world.

The highlight on the day that we arrived was water buffalo fights held in a muddy clearing not far from the site of the funeral ceremonies. Two were paired off against each other at a time. Men, one with an Instamatic camera dangling from his neck, and boys prodded the beasts into action. Even then, most of the buffalos seemed intent on avoiding a confrontation. It usually took a lot of coaxing to get the buffalos to lock horns. When they did, the animals rubbed each other's snouts into the *padi* until one finally gave up and dashed off in another direction, scattering everyone who was in its path.

We returned to the village the next day to find hundreds more guests had arrived and many more pigs and more buffalos chewing cud, oblivious to the torment in store for them. Throughout the morning and into the afternoon, women in black clothes and richly-colored veils flecked with gold, red and purple, paraded back-and-forth under the pavilion that contained the coffins. The processions were interrupted only by feasting. We were offered unappetizing plates of barbecued pig, with black bristles still sticking out of some of the slabs of meat, and tall bamboo tubes foaming at their mouths with

Pop art portraits of the legendary parents of the Minahasan people of North Sulawesi enliven an archway outside the city of Manado (above). A young Makassarese woman (far right) wears her traditional attire with an air of grace and delicacy.

balok, known in other parts of Indonesia as *tuak*, a potent alcoholic brew distilled from fermented rice or palm. Kal ate, I drank.

The slaughter occurred that afternoon. The pigs, already in noisy, agitated agony under the hot sun, were carried on bamboo poles on the shoulders of pairs of men to the funerary pavilion, then taken out to the back. There, old and young men slit the pigs' throats and inserted sharp hollow bamboo tubes in their necks to catch the gushes of blood. It was evident from the intensifying shrieks that the animals were dying horribly painfully. The sound of their death throes became unbearably intense.

But it had to be done. The rules of *Aluk Tomate* require sacrifices to allow the soul to depart from the temporal body via the head, an exit that the Torajan's believe rumples the hair of the corpse. The chronicles that govern *Aluk Todolo* describe the death of a Torajan woman:

> "When she reaches the end of her span of life, then thou shalt go upwards, out of the crown of the head of the puppet clay, and take thy departure, with thy group members to the edge of the firmament at the top of the mountain. When she comes to the absolute point of her physical life, then shalt thou rise up out of her skull, and return to the crown of the hill, to the place from whence the rain moves, with the ones with whom thou art bound in one community."

Kendari, the capital of Southeast Sulawesi, the southeastern prong of the island, has given its name to internationally-renowned silver filigree. This style of spinning delicate threads of precious metal into artistic works of jewelry was devised in the 1920s by a Kendari goldsmith named A. Woei. His technique was picked up and elaborated upon by an artisan in Ujung Pandang, Machmud Tahir, who worked in silver. Tahir created modern motifs like flowers for lady's brooches, buttons and braces and sculptures in the shape of Torajan houses and *pinisi* schooners that caused a sensation at the 1964 New York Art Festival. A lack of capital for boosting production and low earnings for artisans, however, now threatens the future of the craft. Southeast Sulawesi is also known as the home of a nomadic

Donny Tampemawa, an employee of the North Sulawesi tourist office and an avid bodybuilder, appears hardly winded after climbing to the top of Mt. Lokon above Tomohon for a view into the smouldering crater of the active volcano. The classical cone shape of the volcano is a beautiful, if ominous, part of the scenery around Manado.

group of sea gypsies called the Bajau, who live in shifting settlements on the coast and on many islands that are part of the province.

Central Sulawesi, like Southeast Sulawesi, is an underpopulated and underexplored province of raw beauty with a wild coastline of bays and inlets and a sparkling lake called Poso. It also encompasses the Banggai archipelago which dribbles off to the east into the Sula Islands in the Moluccas. Giant Easter Island-style stone megaliths of unknown origin have been discovered in the Bada Valley. Daisy Hadmoko, Indonesia's foremost travel authority, frankly told me that the people of the Central Sulawesi were the warmest, most hospitable, she had ever met during her decades of travel in the archipelago.

I found the people of North Sulawesi equally charming. Although the province is the island's smallest — a thread of a peninsula nearly 800 kilometers long and no more than 50-kilometers wide — it makes up for its size with a sophistication and élan that have made it one of Indonesia's most advanced provinces. The 2.5-million people are largely Minahasans who attribute their origins to legendary warriors like Toar and Lumimuut, the local equivalents of Adam and Eve, whose portraits enliven one of the gateways to the provincial capital, Manado. As the myth goes, Lumimuut, who comes off looking like an Amazon Wonder Woman in portraits, was born from a stone, washed by the sea, heated by the sun and impregnated by the west wind. She gave birth to Toar and later married him. The Minahasans are their offspring. Minahasa means "the united" and is believed to have referred to a confederation of tribes formed in early times to protect the community against rival groups.

Ninety per cent of the people are Protestants and we found the sound of church bells as common in North Sulawesi as the amplified prayer calls of mosques in other parts of the country. Manado's women are consistently ranked by other Indonesians as the archipelago's most attractive, probably because of their fair complexions. Indonesians never let us forget that when we told them we had been to Manado. "Beautiful women. Perhaps you can find a wife," then they would launch into the usual ranking: Manado, prettiest; Yogya, second; Madurese, best lovers. There was a great deal of intermarriage with the Dutch in North Sulawesi.

Not only did that produce light skins but what I found to be the nation's most westernized people.

Manado, on the coconut palm-encrusted northern tip of the northern peninsula is a clean, cosmopolitan town of about a quarter-million people. Flowering hibiscus, bougainvillea, frangipani, allamanda and citrus trees color and gently perfume the wide, well-maintained streets. The classically cone-shaped Lokon volcano looms behind the city above an arc of mountains that is also lush with vegetation.

We spent halcyon days in Manado. We smiled at the young women and rode up bushy mountains through torrents of rain in a jeep driven by an employee of the local tourist office, Donny Tampemawa, whose shirts appeared to be glued to his massive pectorals and biceps. We circumnavigated placid Lake Tondano in the jeep, bouncing through quaint waterside villages full of laughing children and bored dogs, stopping to dip our toes into hot springs and sip murky mineral water from a well sunk in the middle of someone's house, and smiled at pretty women. We dodged raindrops in a graveyard of megalithic *waruga*, big tombstones sculpted with reptiles, fright faces and animals that never existed, where the ancients interrred their dead in crouching positions. We took time out to dine on local delicacies such as scorchingly-spiced fried dog, forest rat and fruit bat.

By far, our best times in Manado were those spent with Loky Herlambang cruising across the glassy waters of Bunaken island in his Nusantara Diving Club's swift, motorized outriggers and swimming in gaudy gardens of coral and undulating anemones under the trained eyes of Elly and Ona, Loky's young female scuba diving instructors. The seas off Bunaken Island are notable for cliffs of coral that plunge in sheer dropoffs to depths of a hundred meters. After the experienced divers returned from the deep and I flippered back to the narrow vessel after snorkeling in the shallows, we motored to a sandy clearing on the island, cut off from the world by palm trees and big boulders, and picnicked.

A few hours later, after the nitrogen had cleared from the divers' bloodstreams and the beer from our brains, we waded through the shallows back to the outriggers. I stepped carefully, wearing my cloth sandals, my apprehension kindled by the group's talk of deadly-poisonous stone fish and sea snakes.

We returned to the reefs for another session the following day. The only irritation during our final dive was a swarm of tiny pink jellyfish that surrounded the cone as we were all surfacing. We ejected ourselves out of the water like sounding whales, our bodies covered with prickly scarlet welts. John Bradford, a Canadian employed in Jakarta who was diving with the group, said he had seen a stone fish swimming about ten meters down.

But venomous creatures had caused little trouble since Bunaken, under Loky's able, ambitious guidance, had begun to attract foreign divers in the mid-seventies. In fact, he said the only casualty had occurred early in 1985 and some local people blamed it on ghosts angered by the tourists who had invaded their watery domain. The victim was a skilled French diver and doctor of hyperbaric medicine.

"The doctor was tested up to 100 meters. We don't know what happened to him," Loky recalled. "He went out with a group that included his wife who was also an expert scuba diver. There were four altogether including one of my instructors. The dive seemed routine, then suddenly one of the group was gone. When they came up, my boy dived again to see if the doctor could have gone off with the other group. They said no. My instructor swam for 400 meters at 40 feet. There was no sign of the man."

"A search-and-rescue team looked for the doctor for three days and went down 70 meters. Some Americans on the search were upset. They thought diving at those depths was suicidal. But we were determined to do everything possible to discover what happened to the man. Yet we never found a trace of him."

"I later recalled what the doctor had told me after returning from his first dive at Bunaken. He said he had gone down 40 or 60 meters and had seen a beautiful red object that he had tried pick up. A beautiful red object! At that depth, it's impossible to see the color red. I believe he must have been hallucinating and that maybe he tried go deeper the next day and hallucinated again until he became lost and no longer knew up from down," Loky said.

"The local people have another explanation. Many of them are still superstitious about things that live in the ocean depths. They believe the red object was a ghost, a ghost that lured the doctor back. When he entered the water the next day, they say, the doctor simply vanished."

A man gathers some greens for his huge water buffalo (right).
The pink blotches identify the animal as a sacred buffalo, the
highest form of sacrifice, slaughtered in honor of the deceased
during the spectacular funerals held in Torajaland.

Chapter Eight

Last Frontiers

*After investigating Canoe Races, Spices, egg-eating
Eels and a haunted Crown in the Moluccas;
man-eating Crocodiles, Cannibals, the Fate of
Michael Rockefeller, and Snow in Irian Jaya;
the Adventures of our exhausted
Chroniclers come to a pleasant End.*

The faces of the villagers of Banda Neira wrinkled inquisitively as the strangers from Jakarta climbed down from the roof of the Maulana Inn where they were installing an odd metal saucer-shaped contraption. Des Alwi, the venerable benefactor of the Banda Islands (a remote part of the larger Moluccas group) affectionately known to all as *"Om* (Uncle) Des," had a surprise in store for the islanders as he often did when he returned home from months of traveling the world on business trips.

Banda Neira, a miniscule town on a microscopic island of 8,000 people, has a few inns, most of them owned by Des, some restaurants and a U-Bix Copy Service. (If an island in the furthest corner of the Indonesian archipelago has anything, it has a photocopy service, usually several. The bureaucracy is fond of official documents, lots of them, that must be filled out in triplicate, quadruplicate or more.) Om Des had brought some extraordinary things to the Banda Islands: airplanes, electrical generators, scuba-diving tanks. But no one had quite seen anything like the device on the roof of the inn.

Its installation was part of an auspicious occasion in October, 1985. Om Des had flown in a coterie of important guests to the gravel runway that spans the entire width of Banda Neira. They included Ibu Hatta and Ibu Sjahrir, the wives of Indonesia's former Vice President and first Prime Minister respectively; the secretary of the present Vice-President; the Dutch Ambassador to Indonesia; the Governor of the Moluccas islands; and, on a less illustrious scale, Kal and me.

The main event was the opening of an old colonial home that Des and the islanders had renovated and turned into a museum. The former Vice President, Mohammad Hatta, had lived in the home from 1936 to 1942 when he and the Republic's first Prime Minister, Sutan Sjahrir, were exiled to Banda by the Dutch administration for their anti-colonial activities. During their stay, the two men befriended local families and began tutoring some of their children. Among them was Des. He was only eight-years-old when the two important men arrived. But the friendship between the young boy and the two revolutionary leaders took root and proved fruitful.

"They were friends, my good friends," Des said. The new Hatta Museum is one token of his appreciation. At the dedication ceremony, Des gave a humorous speech about his relationship with Mohammad Hatta and Sjahrir and led a tour of the museum. Afterwards, we followed Des back to his residential compound. The gates were always thrown open to anyone in town who felt like wandering into the grounds. The compound was on the edge of a sparkling lagoon where, against the background of the perfect volcanic cone of 670-meter Gunung Api, the "Fire Mountain" on the next island, four brilliantly-painted *kora-kora* outrigger canoes floated. Each canoe had 36 men, some bare-chested, some wearing T-shirts that identified them as a team representing Neira or one of the neighboring islands. The men were singing ancient war chants in the old language of the islands to drumbeats, warming up their biceps and psyching themselves to paddle in what Des was calling the inaugural running of the Bunga Hatta Cup Kora-Kora Race.

Then, the men paddled off until their canoes disappeared into the open seas around a bend in the island. Ten minutes later, the canoes reappeared at top speed, two almost even in front, two far behind. The men's arms pumped the oars like pistons to the

The charcoal gray walls of Fort Duurstede (preceding pages), probably built four centuries ago by the Portuguese but later fortified by the Dutch, are a stark contrast to the blinding tropical colors of Saparua Island in the Moluccas, the "Spice Islands". At left, a pretty smile from a young woman of Ambon.

rhythm of drumbeats and the canoes whooshed past cheering crowds at a nifty 15 knots. The paddlers from Ai Island crossed the finish line first. Yet, they hardly seemed winded when Des presented the team with a weighty trophy while a band assembled on the bank played "Roll Out the Barrel." For some reason, the tune did not sound out of place on an island half-a-world away from the nearest polka hall.

That night I retired early, but I heard partying long into the night as Des led his family and guests in the *Hawaiian Wedding Song, Before the Next Teardrop Falls* and an assortment of Indonesian and Moluccan tunes. Des is a Muslim, like more than half of the people of the Banda Islands, and there was no liquor at the party. Indonesians can keep the adrenalin flowing long into the night without it.

A homemade wooden yacht was waiting to take us across to Lonthor Island, only a few kilometers off Neira's southern flank, the next morning. Des, ever the entertainer, boarded, wearing electric blue rubber diving bootees, a batik shirt and a Japanese soldier's cap apparently rescued from World War II, the kind with floppy, beagle ears. The vessel listed to one side then the other under the shifting weight of too many passengers as it puttered across the placid waters, above tangled beds of colored coral a couple of meters below. A gaily-dressed delegation was already gathering on shore to greet the honored guests. The tide was low and there was no dock, so Ibu Hatta, Ibu Sjahrir and several others transferred to a metal dinghy. But the dinghy soon scraped bottom too. The men of the village had a solution for that. They waded out and picked up the small boat, occupants and all, and carried it ashore.

Lonthor village had been tidied and was blooming with pink oleander. The people welcomed us with a *Cakalele*, a spirited war dance. A guidebook put out by the tourist development board of the Moluccas described it as being "danced by men in traditional war costumes, looking indigenous and native." Actually, the nine young men who gyrated and shimmey-shaked enthusiastically on the dusty main street were dressed in the manner of Portuguese explorers of the 16th century in medieval outfits of red, green, black and yellow trimmed in white and they wore steel helmets and carried narrow shields.

The *Cakalele* is performed only occasionally and then only after a series of ritual preparations.

The crew of a canoe, revered as a magically-powerful heirloom, primes itself for the Bung Hatta Cup Kora-Kora Race held on a sparkling lagoon in the Banda Islands. After long centuries during which the islands were plundered by the Dutch for their spices, the men flaunt their allegiance to the red-and-white flag of the Republic of Indonesia.

Brandishing sharp metal-tipped spears, machetes and shields, men of Lonthor
high-step-it in a spirited war dance of the islands called the *Cakalele* (above and top left).
Their costumes, especially the metal helmets (bottom left), exhibit the unmistakable
influence of the Portuguese explorers who came to the Moluccas in the 16th century.

Beforehand, holy men "open" the village to spirits as well as to human visitors by taking offerings of betel nuts to several sacred locations. On Lonthor, there were 11 such locations. Each was believed to be the tomb of former leaders killed by the Dutch and were considered gateways to the other world. Even the accouterments for the dance, as we later discovered on Ai Island, are considered *pusaka*, magical heirlooms. They were kept behind curtains in a special room that has an altar full of offerings where incense was kept burning and the Islamic holy book, the Koran, was opened.

We followed the *Cakalele* dancers down the narrow main street. It was lined on either side by girls and boys wearing red-and-white scout uniforms who saluted solemnly until we passed. Then they broke rank and closed in behind us for a better look. As if time-released, a flock of birds that looked like white doves but were probably terns, fluttered gracefully above the procession.

Later, we hiked up steep flights of stairs on a ridge overlooking the town to the ruins of a stone fort that was rapidly disappearing under pandanus and banyan trees and thickening clumps of vines and lianas. Underneath was what remained of Fort Hollandia, erected in 1621 by Jan Pieterszoon Coen. From the bluff, across the rapidly receding lagoon

back on Neira Island, we could also see the soot-colored walls of Fort Belgica, built in 1611 by Pieter Both, Governor-General of the Dutch East Indies, and the lighter, lower-lying bulwarks of Fort Nassau, built in 1609 by Dutch Admiral Pieterszoon Verhoeven on foundations laid by the Portuguese. It was hard to believe, but the brooding remains of the fortresses were proof that these serene islands, so far from anywhere, were once the source of the Netherlands' wealth and power and the scene of violent battles for supremacy. History's fabled Spice Islands were the only place in the world at that time where nutmeg encased in its prized fleece, mace, literally grew on trees. Along with cloves and peppers from Ternate, Tidore and other islands in the north Moluccas nutmeg was then worth its weight in gold, according to George Masselman, author of the definitive study, *The Cradle of Colonialism*. So important were the islands that Run, little more than a coral outcropping, was an integral part of the Treaty of Breda of 1667. The treaty gave the Dutch the legal right to Run and its nutmeg groves. In return, England received a chunk of real estate off the east coast of the New World now called Manhattan.

The forts in the Banda group were built not only to protect the islands against other colonial powers like the Portuguese and the British, but as protec-

A lone fisherman, engulfed by the unimaginable blues of the Banda Sea, rows ashore on Ai Island (left). A pair of goats (above), soon to be turned into curry, and sea turtles, destined to become soup, purchased from the villagers of Ai, take a boat ride to Banda Neira for a feast prepared for visiting VIPs.

Boats are the major transportation link between the stunning islands of the Moluccas. Above, two lovely vessels sail past Gunung Api in the Bandas. Below, a ferry boat with a full load of passengers passes a fishing *bagan* off Haruku Island.

tion against the islanders themselves. From the beginning, relations between the Dutch and the Bandanese were strained. The Dutch merchants complained that the *orang kaya*, the local leaders who controlled nutmeg production, reneged on promises to deliver goods at agreed prices and juggled weights, mixing cheaper nutmegs with more valued mace. Likewise, the Bandanese were not happy with the heavy Dutch woolens and damasks, useless in their sweltering climate, and trinkets they received for the spices. Traditional Javanese, Arab and Indian traders, even the Portuguese, brought them more useful barter: food staples like rice and sago and light batik cloth from Java and calicoes from India, and Chinese porcelain, knives, copper gongs and medicine. The Bandanese may have been more dismayed if they knew that their spices were sold in Amsterdam for 320 times the purchase price.

Dutch insistence that the Bandanese trade exclusively with the VOC, the Dutch East Indies Company, and the construction of Fort Nassau aroused the ire of the *orang kaya*. In 1609, armed islanders attacked a group of VOC officials who had come to Neira to squeeze more concessions out of the local people. More than 30 Hollanders were killed. In retaliation, Coen sent more than 2,000 soldiers to the Bandas in 1621 to subdue the people. Historian Hall said that the Dutch "completely depopulated" the Bandas. Many people were slaughtered, others deported. Forty-four *orang kaya* were beheaded and quartered by Japanese samurai who worked as mercenaries for the Dutch, an episode recalled in a bloody painting in one of the museums of Neira. Their heads were stuck on bamboo poles and displayed in public as a warning against further uprisings. Afterwards, Coen divided the Bandas into 68 *perken*, parcels, that were licensed to Dutch planters called *perkeniers*.

"Maluku was blessed by the lord with its spices. But the blessing turned out to be a curse. These islands have suffered very much simply because they were rich," lamented Josef Mustika, the secretary of the office of Indonesia's Vice President and a retired Major General of the Armed Forces, who was among the VIPs at Des' party. Mustika and his attractive wife had both been born in Ambon.

Nutmeg production and profits peaked around the beginning of the 18th century, but then began to decline as the market became saturated with spices from seedlings that were transplanted to British-controlled plantations in Ceylon and the Malay Peninsula. The Banda Islands reverted to relative obscurity. But Coen's cruelty towards the people of the Bandas has not been forgotten.

"Even by 17th century standards, Coen went too far," Dutch Ambassador François Van Dongen told us. Van Dongen, the only Dutchman in the party, came in for some good-natured ribbing from Des and other Indonesians. Harry Kawilarang, a journalist from Jakarta, walked around wearing a T-shirt with the words, "Only a VOC remnant."

As the Dutch Ambassador and other VIPs began leaving the day after visiting Lonthor, the islanders' interest in the men from Jakarta who were fiddling with the gadgets on the roof of the inn intensified. Eventually, they put a protective beach umbrella over the equipment and word got out that the big event was about to happen. Crowds began gathering before dusk. Vendors laid out blankets along the dirt roadside from which they sold peanuts, sweets, cigarettes and other goods by candlelight. Soon, the men from Jakarta struggled out of the hotel and up the ledge to the marketplace across the street lugging a huge, heavy box with the letters JVC printed on the sides. The villagers, wide-eyed, moved in closer as a big square screen was pulled from the box and set on a table. A switch was flicked. Television had come to Banda.

The Bandanese are fairly worldly, given their turbulent history of contact with the West, yet they waited until 1985 for the first television link with the rest of the world made possible by Des Alwi's satellite dish. Government-generated electricity only arrived in 1983. That is just how remote and isolated the Bandas are among the islands collectively known as the Moluccas, or Maluku in Indonesian.

An accurate count of the number of Moluccas islands does not seem to exist. One figure that writers favor is 999. Geographers agree that the Moluccas encompass about 88,000 square kilometers of land that has been diced and sprinkled around 763,911 square kilometers of tepid seas on Indonesia's northern frontier. They are divided into three administrative provinces. North Maluku includes Ternate and Tidore and the large island of

The religious bent of the Moluccas was also influenced by the long colonial presence, particularly in Ambon where the majority of the people are Christians. In parts of the island, banners proclaim biblical slogans and paintings of Christ are found on the walls of buildings and even decorate a leftover Dutch army bunker near the village of Tulehu.

Halmahera. Southeast Maluku includes the very isolated Kai and Aru Islands and the Tanimbars. And Central Maluku includes Ambon and the Bandas. The total population of the Moluccas was estimated at little more than 1.6 million in 1985.

Central Maluku accounts for nearly half the land area and population. One of the largest but least explored islands of the province, Ceram, has mountain ranges up to 3,000-meters high and is home to the feared Alfuru tribe. The nucleus of all the Moluccas, a smidgin of an island under Ceram's southwestern corner, is Ambon, one of the first of the Spice Islands colonized by Westerners. The Portuguese arrived in Ambon (the island consists of two parallel peninsulas, Hitu and Leitimor, connected by a narrow isthmus) early in the 16th century. A passage in *The Chronicles of Hitu*, written in 1646, describes the Ambonese' first impression of Europeans:

> "One day the people ... encountered a boat full of human creatures the likes of whom they had never seen before. Their bodies were white and their eyes resembled cats' eyes. They were asked questions, but they did not speak the local language."

Although the greatest quantities of cloves were grown in Ternate and Tidore, two islands 480 kilometers to the north, and nutmeg and mace production was centered in the Bandas 160 kilometers south, Ambon, with an excellent harbor cradled by the hilly peninsulas, became a base of operations, first for the Portuguese then for the Dutch. It has continued to grow in importance within the archipelago, while Ternate, Tidore and the Bandas have reverted to sleepy backwaters.

Nearly a quarter-million people live on Ambon, a major nexus on the archipelago's air and sea routes. Like all of the islands of the Moluccas, it is pleasant, slow-paced and reminiscent of Polynesia. The mixing of ethnic Malays and Australoids has produced an indigenous people with a South Pacific look. Many of the women have shining black cascades of hair and extremely tan skin, while the men are generally bigger and hairier than Indonesians of purely Malay descent. More than half the people of Ambon are Christians. One of the first influential missionaries was Saint Francis Xavier, the Basque priest who was one of the founders of the Jesuits. He

the south coast where we found the walls of buildings, facades of homes and even a Dutch shore bunker left over from the war of independence painted with portraits of Jesus and his apostles. A banner across a side street read "In Jesus we are all brothers" on one side and "Jesus is the trunk, we are the branches" on the other.

The Ambonese, like Indonesians of all faiths, practice a Christianity tinged with the ancient ways. Some of the old lore centers around a clear spring in the village of Waai just down the road from the Jesus banner. Swarms of eels inhabit the rocks and live under the concrete eaves bordering the spring. The caretaker was 43-year-old Baldus Bakarbessy, who said his family had long been keepers of the eels.

Baldus sauntered into the clear shallow spring and thumped the surface of the water with his thumb. He tried several variations before he got his thumb just right. Out of the depths snaked an eel that was at least two-meters long. It cautiously approached Baldus who cracked open a hen's egg and let the yellow yolk ooze into the water. The eel slurped it up, circled several times as if expecting applause, then swam back into the stony recesses.

"There are more than 100 eels in the spring. Some are very old. I know one that has been here 66 years," Baldus said. We had heard rumblings that the people of Waai and other Ambonese believed the eels were sacred, the repositories of the souls of important ancestors, but none of the Christians in our entourage would admit to such superstitions.

established missions in the Moluccas and won converts to Catholicism in Ambon, Ternate and Morotai in 1546 and 1547. By the 18th century, there were 60,000 Catholics in the Spice Islands.

Christians and Muslims were once at loggerheads with each other, partially as a result of clashes between the Europeans and the Moluccan sultans and groups that controlled the spices. But a body of common law called *pela* developed that eased tensions and improved relations between religious groups in the Moluccas. Paramita Abdurachman, a gracious woman and an acknowledged authority on the Moluccas, attributes the origin of *pela* to head-hunting days when it was used as a mechanism for restoring peace between warring tribes or villages. From those beginnings she said, *pela* developed into a formal form of peace treaty always concluded with a ceremonial oath-taking that created sacred bonds between various groups. "Each form of *pela* nowadays differs from village to village, crossing religious affiliations and *uli* (brotherhoods or clans) and geographical boundaries, but always keeping the cosmic order in balance," Paramita said. Today, partly because of *pela*, Christians and Muslims live in relative harmony in the Moluccas.

Quaint Dutch churches can be found throughout the island. But Christian influence is strongest along

Ternate may be the most physically stunning of all Indonesia's landfalls. Small, only 40 square kilometers and just nine kilometers in diameter, Ternate is almost all mountain, the luxuriant green and fitful, 1,720-meter Gamalama volcano that sweeps straight out of the aqua seas. Ternate's sister island, Tidore, 50 square kilometers dominated by a 1,739-meter volcano, is almost a twin. Veteran travelers say Ternate and Tidore rival Bora-Bora in the South Pacific for tropical splendor.

When we landed at Ternate airport, passing clumps of cloud dusted the sooty vent of Gamalama which looked capable of blowing its top at any moment. The volcano's lower slopes were lush with tall stalks of bamboo, banana, coconut, durian, mango and other fruit trees and stands of spice trees.

Most of the horizon was filled by Halmahera, the largest of the islands in the Moluccas, a sparsely-inhabited wilderness that is the home of the star of the bird world, the *cenderawasih* or bird of paradise. Halmahera is a twisted pinwheel of peninsulas that looks like a small version of Sulawesi on maps.

Ternate Town, huddled in Gamalama's shadow on the water's edge, was a quiet jumble of Chinese shophouses and the remnants of moldering medieval bulwarks, where vehicles moved slowly and stopped at crosswalks, a rare phenomenon I had observed nowhere else in the archipelago. The stars provided more illumination than street lamps at night. Sleeping in a shabby hotel in a town tacked on the side of an ominous volcano was hardly a unique experience in Indonesia. But on my first night on Ternate, my dreams of running from rivers of boiling lava were enhanced when at precisely 12:45 p.m. I felt the bed sway. When I woke up, I realized it was not just the bed but the entire room that was moving. It was just another routine earth tremor.

A tour of Ternate was a tour of Eden. Ancient eruptions of Gamalama have pockmarked its slopes with some bottomless craters that had since filled with water and grown fringes of vegetation transforming them into idyllic lagoons with steep cliffs up to 100-meters high in spots. We made a complete circuit on the only road that circumvents the island. The twisted roots of banyan trees seemed to be the only thing holding up the decomposing gate of Fort Nuestra Senõra Del Rosaria south of town. Vegetation had practically buried the rest of the fortification. After stumbling around the rubble, we must have looked thirsty or as if we had a few spare rupiah, because without being asked a sinewy young man shinnied up a palm tree, *parang* in hand. We heard a few whacks then six green coconuts as big as bowling balls thudded to the ground at our feet. The man shinnied down, deftly hacked at each gourd a few more times, and handed a coconut to each of our party. Liquid trickled down my neck as I threw back my head and eagerly poured the sweet, cooling coconut milk into my mouth.

North of town, the paved road cut through a solid trail of black boulders, petrified lava from an eruption of Gamalama in 1737 that left a path of destruction from the peak to the sea. The people of Ternate call the lava trail, Batu Angus, "scorched rock". Our guides, a van full of tourist department people, official and otherwise, pointed up the blackened path to the peak and pointed out that Gamalama had three peaks named Arafat, Medina and Mecca for Islamic holy places. Undoubtedly, the domineering mountain had a mystical hold on

Indonesia's Moluccas islands boast all of the elements travelers expect of a tropical paradise, including spectacular birds that fly wild through the palms. Among the best-known species are the black-crested cockatoo (left) and the bird of paradise (above).

the people of Ternate, but Omar Ammari, a self-employed cicerone called into service by the local government, was a fervent Muslim who evaded questions about local legends and beliefs.

At the next lagoon, cockatoos chattered in the branches of spice trees. Evergreens produce the dried, unopened flower buds that made Ternate and its neighbors the epicenter of international intrigue. Once prized for their use in medicine and dentistry, and as a flavoring, fragrance and breath freshener, cloves were known long before Europeans arrived in the Moluccas. In fact, ancient records indicate that courtiers of the Han Dynasty used cloves to sweeten their breath as early as the third century B.C. and annals of the Tang Dynasty mention "*Mi-li-ku.*" The spice reached Egypt in the second century A.D. and its reputation spread through Europe during the Middle Ages touching off the great search for more of it.

The Portuguese followed the scent of cloves to Ternate in 1511 with the explorers Francisco Serrão and Antonio d'Abreu and managed to maintain a base there until 1575 when the Sultan expelled them. Although the Portuguese established a new fortress across the channel in Tidore, their main base became Ambon. An expedition of Spain's Fernando Magellan put in at Tidore in 1521 and England's Sir Francis Drake visited Ternate in 1579 during his round-the-world voyage. But the presence of the Spanish and English in the Moluccas was brief.

The Dutch arrived on the scene comparatively late. A trading fleet commanded by Jacob van Neck, Wijbrand van Wirwijck and Jacob van Heemskerck put in at Ambon with a fleet of ships from five Dutch companies in 1598, three years after Cornelis de Houtman's expedition got as far as Java. According to historian M.C. Ricklefs, they returned with "enough spices to show a 400 per cent profit." Competing trading companies merged to form the VOC, which occupied Ambon in 1605 setting the stage for Coen's vicious subjugation of the Bandas. From Ambon, the Dutch pushed into Ternate and through force and connivance drove the last Spaniards from Tidore and Ternate in 1663, solidifying their monopoly of the spice trade. But the heyday of the fabled spice islands was relatively brief. The British and French successfully transplanted cloves and other spices to their colonies in Ceylon, Malaysia and Africa. By the 18th century, spices were declining in economic importance and attention shifted to other parts of the archipelago.

Cloves are still cultivated, however. About 500,000 productive trees are spread out across about 120,000 hectares on Ternate, Tidore, Makian, Bacan and Motir. One gargantuan tree on Ternate, said to be

350 years old, still yields as much as 150 kilograms of cloves a year. But clove production in the Spice Islands has been surpassed by Zanzibar and other parts of Africa. Ironically, Indonesia, once the world's premier exporter of spices, now imports about 30,000 tons of cloves annually for use in its flourishing *kretek* cigarette industry which favors Madagascar cloves.

Another remnant of Ternate's glorious days is the palace of its long line of sultans, a brooding hulk of stone overlooking the harbor from a grassy promontory in town. If any place on Ternate was haunted, we figured the palace was it. We were right.

Late one afternoon, we signed the guest book, one of the rituals of travel in Indonesia, doffed our shoes and walked in. The palace has been transformed into a museum. Suits of Dutch armor, royal regalia and the like are displayed in its musty halls. There was something peculiar about the main chamber. Arranged on a square of white linen on the floor held down by seashells at the corners were bottles of water, petals of the *menuru* flower and a bowl of sandalwood ash. On the wall hung an oil painting of a young man in a military uniform, seated with a sword in his hand. The man's face had a haunted look and his eyes made me shudder. But the eeriest element of the painting was the man's crown. It was indistinctly-shaped with a crescent studded with diamonds on its anterior, tassles of rubies, sapphires, pearls and diamonds — and a plume of what appeared to be hair that spouted from the back of the crown almost to the man's shoulders.

Ammari said the portrait was of Iskandar Muhamad Djabir Syah, the last Sultan of Ternate who had died in 1975. He evaded questions about the strange crown and the paraphernalia on the floor of the room, mumbling something about superstitions. The curator of the museum, Ferdinan Nyong, a young man with an afro hairstyle, goatee and mustache, was more frank. He said the flowers and sandalwood were offerings to the spirit of Ternate's first sultan, Masyur, which according to some believers resided in the very crown in the portrait. The hair at the back of the crown was that of Masyur himself, Ferdinan said. Masyur's hair had continued growing during the centuries and had to be trimmed in special ceremonies every few years.

"The color of the hair has changed through the years to match the hair color of the king who wears it," Ferdinan said. "The legends say the crown came down from *kayangan*, or heaven, which is a special place somewhere between the sky and air. Many people here still believe in the magical strength of the crown and the spirits of the island."

Young Indonesians remove stems from a freshly-picked batch of cloves (left), the aromatic bud that led to the colonial invasion of Ternate, Tidore and the other Spice Islands and was the foundation upon which the Dutch mercantile empire was built. Another spice indigenous to the Moluccas, nutmeg, grows with a flaming red fleece of valuable mace (above).

In fact, during a particularly violent eruption of Gamalama in 1983, the son of the man in the portrait, Sultan Muda Mudhafa Syah, the man who would be king now and who is a member of parliament, returned from Jakarta. A festival was held and people prayed to the crown. Then the sultan donned his father's traditional clothes. Sixteen *kora-kora* war canoes gathered in the harbor. The sultan was alone in the lead canoe with 12 rowers. Eight other VIPs boarded other canoes. The *kora-kora* procession circumnavigated the island once while the people continued praying. Gamalama stopped erupting soon afterwards.

"The crown is kept in there," Ferdinan said. He pointed to a curtain. Behind it was a door barricaded by a table. We asked if we could see the crown and photograph it. A petite, effeminate man in a turban and long white cloak suddenly appeared. He said we needed special permission to view the crown — and the key to the door of the room.

We spent most of the next morning flitting from office-to-office and house-to-house. Eventually, we got an okay to photograph the mysterious crown. Locating the key to the room where it was kept proved trickier. After several stops, including one where we were joined by the man authorized to use the key, we were told the little man in the turban had the key, but he was nowhere to be found. At yet another bungalow, the key apparently materialized although we never saw it.

Back at the palace, Ferdinan set the mood for our encounter with the crown of Ternate by telling us of the strange occurrences he had experienced:

"In 1982, a man from Ambon helped us prepare for the opening of the museum. He came in under the pavilion at the back when he arrived just like you. Suddenly, two big black snakes were at our feet, hissing at us. It was as if they had just fallen out of nowhere, from the roof beams or something. When people tried to catch them, the snakes weren't there. I'm a Christian, but that made me worry.

"A few days later, we rearranged some of the furniture in the Sultan's bedroom where the crown is kept. The man from Ambon thought the room would look better if we turned the canopy bed around, facing another direction. That night I slept on the veranda with some of the laborers. The door to the Sultan's bedroom was locked. But all night long we heard noises as if somebody was inside.

"The next morning, we entered the bedroom. We didn't dare go in at night. Inside, we found the bed facing the way it had been before we arranged the room. Somehow the bed had turned itself around during the night! That really worried us.

As Ferdinan was finishing his tales, we too heard noises emanating from behind the curtain that veiled the door to the bedroom. Then the curtain was pulled aside and the door opened. The knee-high table blocked our entrance. We leaned over and peered into the gloom from behind it.

A few feet beyond the door was a case covered by a white cloth. In front of that was a table of offerings and an antique Koran opened to reveal beautifully-scripted Arabic characters. Against the wall on the left was the grand old canopy bed of Ferdinan's tale. It was draped with a white lace curtain and was made up with fresh linens and two bolsters as if it was still used every night.

Then all eyes turned to the covered case. A man, unpretentiously dressed in a long-sleeve batik shirt, pulled back the white cloth. Underneath was a glass case. Inside was the crown.

We were not the least bit disappointed. Its gold was tarnished and its gems had lost their luster, but the crown looked thoroughly haunted. At the back, sprouting right from the metal rim, was a matted black growth that looked like a shock of greasy, unwashed hair. Everyone began speaking in reverential whispers, including me.

"A professor from John Hopkins University in the United States examined the crown a few years ago. He handled the hair and pronounced it human," Ferdinan said with a convincing flourish.

Meanwhile, Kal had fetched his Polaroid. He leaned across the coffee table barrier as far into the bedroom as he could and pushed the button. Out came a square of instant film. The image seemed to well up more slowly than usual, but a picture of the crown did appear. And so did an ectoplasmic white blotch just to the side of the crown. I called the apparent flaw to Kal's attention. He squinted at the photograph. "Must be a reflection from the flash," he said. I was not the only one present who was not convinced by Kal's explanation. I looked at Ferdinan. Ferdinan looked at me. His brow was furrowed. He had yet another tale to tell.

As in much of Indonesia, the Islamic practices of Ternate have a mystical side rooted in pre-Islamic religions. Some islanders believe a spirit dwells in the crown of the island's former sultans (above top) and that the strange growth on its back rim is human hair. An old Koran (bottom) is among the sacred heirlooms in the guarded room in the palace where the ancient crown is kept.

Modern and primitive cultures meet in Irian Jaya where most people lived in Stone Age isolation from the 20th century until recent years. A helicopter delivers supplies and medicine to a Damal village in the rugged Sudirman highlands (preceding pages). In most places, rickety suspension bridges pieced together from rattan rigging and tree limbs are the only means of crossing the raging rivers of Irian Jaya (above).

During our travels in Indonesia in 1985 to complete our research and photography for this book, Kal and I made our first trip to Irian Jaya. It was the last leg of a long agenda. We sailed from Ambon to Sorong at the far northwestern edge of Irian Jaya aboard the *Km. Rinjani*, one of four impressive passenger vessels specially built in West Germany for use by the state shipping line, Pelni.

After five months of almost constant travel, we treated ourselves to first-class rooms for the overnight passage. The cabin was equipped with color television, radio and a shower with hot and cold running water, far more luxury than we had become accustomed to. The 13,860-ton vessel has five classes, accommodates up to 1,871 passengers, and has 126 crew members including 20 officers.

The next morning we met M.J. Sompie, the *Rinjani's* 55-year-old Manadonese captain, on the bridge of the ship as it cruised at a brisk 21 knots through the Salawati Straits. Moist clouds played on the lush, low mountains of Batanta Island on our left and Salawati on our right.

Captain Somphie said the four giant passenger ships had come into service between 1983 and 1985 and linked the islands of Indonesia all the way from Belawan in northern Sumatra to Jayapura on Indonesia's eastern boundary. "We're beginning to get a lot of Italians, Germans and American passengers. Our Indonesian passengers enjoy watching the Europeans strolling around the decks in their swimsuits," Somphie said.

Captain Somphie sucked on a *kretek* and confidently called out commands in Indonesian for the ship's speed and direction as the *Rinjani* closed in on the port of Sorong on the tuft of the island of New Guinea that the Dutch called Vogelkopf, or Bird's Head. A collection of fishing dugouts parted like the Red Sea as the immense vessel skimmed over the placid waters into the harbor. It eased up to the dock, seven decks far below. A tug named *Bintuni* nudged the vessel's stern into place.

Kal and I enlisted the muscle of two sweating porters who hoisted our heavy bags onto their shoulders. We followed them out the gangway to the wharf where we waded into an ocean of pushing and shoving people. It seemed that the majority of Sorong's 150,000 people had turned out for the *Rinjani's* arrival. Most had the dark skins and features of Melanesians. We were in yet another of Indonesia's many worlds.

There seemed to be little to the town of Sorong. We took a mini-truck in and at a Garuda Airways office learned that a flight was due to leave shortly for Jayapura, Irian Jaya's provincial capital and our target destination. We decided to go for it and the truck took us back to the docks where we bundled our luggage onto a narrow longboat. It was the only way to get to Jefman Airport, which was on an offshore island 30 kilometers from Sorong. Travel logistics were already becoming complicated. The boat sped off, the 40 h.p. Johnson outboards spraying fountains of water behind us.

A brand new F–28 took us to Jayapura. In the rear of the cabin, a cockatoo was engaged in a delightful conversation with itself. The bird belonged to an aircraft maintenance engineer who was aboard. The engineer said the cockatoo's name was Jacob. "Jacob *lapar*. Jacob *lapar*." squawked the bird. *Lapar* is Indonesian for "hungry."

Separated from Jakarta by nearly 3,500 kilometers of seas and islands and by even wider cultural gaps, Jayapura is a drab town in a superb setting in a trough between steep grassy knolls on the north coast of New Guinea that faces the vast sapphire blue Pacific. It is the gateway to Irian Jaya, a part of Indonesia starkly different from the rest of the country in every respect and a land of jolting extremes. The terrain is more contorted and impenetrable, the climate more capricious, the cultures more macabre.

At least three mountains that rise about 5,000 meters are permanently snowcapped — Puncak Jaya, Trikora and Mandala — even though they are only a few degrees from the equator. These peaks are in mountain ranges that severely shelf down to the wave-whipped Arafura Sea of the south coast. Puncak Jaya, just 95 kilometers from the sea, plunges from 5,000 meters to about 300 in the course of only 40 kilometers. The southern Casuarina Coast is a cauldron of swamps of sago, nipah and areca palms and mangrove trees infested with deadly poisonous death adders and man-eating crocodiles 10-meters long, a realm nicknamed "the land of lapping death." There are ravishing birds of paradise whose glamorous tail feathers grow up to a half meter. There are vast areas of people who had no

Women of Irian Jaya paddle two male passengers in a simple canoe hollowed out of a log. The people of the southern Casuarina Coast are expert oarsmen who negotiate their skimpy craft through primordial swamps infested with deadly poisonous snakes and man-eating crocodiles that grow up to 10 meters in length.

contact with the outside world until quite recently (one group was first contacted in 1979) and who engaged in tribal warfare with primitive wooden spears and bows and arrows and practiced ritual cannibalism. There are at least 231 individual languages, some relegated to pockets of only a few hundred people. Irian Jaya is without question Indonesia's last frontier.

Comprising about half of New Guinea, the world's second largest island after Greenland, and assorted smaller islands, Irian Jaya is 410,660 square kilometers of swampland, marsh and massifs. It accounts for 21 per cent of Indonesia's total land mass. As of 1981, its population was 1.2 million, a density of only three per square kilometer. The province sprawls more than 1,200 kilometers from the border with Papua New Guinea to its western reaches and 730 kilometers north to south at its broadest point. Irian Jaya has 31-million hectares of forests that cover 75 per cent of its surface and some 55,000 square kilometers of rivers and lakes. The two longest of its 31 major rivers, the Mamberamo and Digul, are fraught with perilous rapids and waterfalls. Among the largest of its 13 major lake systems are Paniai, formerly the Wissel, and Sentani.

Lake Sentani, in an embrace of rolling hillocks, is absolutely enticing. We were able to endure frequent trips back and forth between Jayapura and the airport at Sentani, a solid hour of driving one way, simply because the road skirted the lake. The scenery took our minds off the fact that we were squashed into a public "taxi," a van with as many as 15 other people and sometimes their pet piglets.

American General Douglas MacArthur enjoyed a spectacular panorama of Sentani from his headquarters situated high on a bluff. From there, he directed portions of his Pacific campaign during World War II. At that time, Jayapura was Hollandia, a Dutch hamlet. The usual merchants and colonial powers had all landed on New Guinea's shores, first the Chinese and Malays, then the Portuguese and Spanish. Britain's famed Captain Cook paid a visit.

The Dutch annexed Irian in 1828. The Japanese raised their flag over New Guinea as part of its Pacific empire in 1942. MacArthur stormed the beaches in April, 1944, drove out the Japanese and transformed Hollandia into a massive staging area for the drive against Japan's stronghold in the

Philippines. The American military presence lingers in Jayapura: on the positive side, relatively good infrastructure; on the negative, hundreds of rusting hulks of landing barges and the city's quonset hut architecture. Shophouses, dwellings, even schools, have been fashioned out of these stark, unattractive semicircles of corrugated iron.

The United States returned sovereignty over Irian to the Dutch after the war, but the Indonesians staked their claim after independence citing historic ties like the Majapahit Empire's inclusion of western New Guinea and the Sultan of Tidore's titles to parts of the island. After military skirmishes in the jungles and years of wrangling in the United Nations, Indonesia was accorded control of Irian in 1963.

The most practical means of getting around Irian Jaya, in fact about the only way of getting around, is by plane. The province may be undeveloped in almost all other respects, but it certainly has more airports than other areas of its size, approximately 250, many hewn from the wilderness by missionaries. Calling some of them airports is stretching it, however. An airstrip directory compiled by the Missionary Aviation Fellowship (MAF) cautions pilots about landing fields with unnervingly curving gradients "from six to 10 to 12 per cent" (on the same strip!) and "straight up a hill." One paragraph

under surface conditions reads: "Very rough! Poor condition. Soft when wet. Grass usually not well cut. Pigs digging up strip in many places."

Tricky air currents, cliffs and mountain peaks permanently concealed in clouds and quirky changes in weather make flying in Irian iffy in small planes, the only kind most airstrips can accommodate. The Indonesian and foreign bush pilots of the province are a gutsy breed, to say the least.

One of the world's great unsolved mysteries is the disappearance of Michael Rockefeller, the son of Nelson, the late American business tycoon. In 1961, at the age of 23, Rockefeller, heir to a fortune, set off on an art-collecting expedition among the Asmat tribe of the south central coastal swamps and never returned. His fate still sparks debate.

Foreigners that had descended on the unsuspecting Asmat at that time had painted the Asmat as savages. A French documentary *The Sky Above, The Mud Below*, vividly depicted a Stone Age culture that thrived on vicious warfare and cannibalism and preternatural rituals that had audiences gasping. In his book *Peace Child*, missionary Don Richardson who worked in the area in the early 1960s portrayed cultures in which treachery was a virtue and people delighted in *tuwai asonai man* which literally means

"fattening with friendship for the slaughter." The Sawuy people, neighbors of the Asmat, cheered Judas as a hero when Richardson tried to tell them the story of the crucifixion of Jesus Christ. Richardson's bestseller told of gruesome orgies where men, women, and children alike participated, wearing cassowary bones in their noses, boars' tusks around their necks, bird of paradise plumes in their hair and warpaint on their faces. The people lived in treehouses at that time, tucked like birdnests as high as 12 meters up in canopies of branches to protect themselves from the relentless jungle vermin and from one another.

Elaborate schemes were developed to lure enemies and "friends" alike into traps. Victims were routinely murdered with spears, bows and arrows and clubs, their bodies butchered to the beat of drum heads made from lizard skin glued on with human blood. The gleeful victors then barbecued the pieces, feasted on the human meat, slurped up the brains, triumphantly displayed the skulls as wall ornaments and, at night, used them as pillows. They gave the jawbones to their girlfriends who proudly wore them around their necks like fine jewelry. Richardson described one particularly loathsome veneration of dead acquaintances called *gefam ason* in which the corpse of a deceased villager is allowed

An armored landing vehicle left over from World War II rusts away in the provincial capital of Jayapura (above). Such craft were used by the Allied Forces of General Douglas MacArthur to storm the Japanese-held beaches. The general directed part of the Pacific campaign from a quonset hut high atop a ridge above Jayapura (left), then called Hollandia by the Dutch colonials.

In the sweltering swamps and cool highlands of the south coast, the people of Irian Jaya still cling to some old customs — including their mode of dress. Women wear hairnets (above) and grass skirts, hunters (right) wear the penis gourd or *koteka*.

to rot in a "gravehouse" in the tropical heat for nine days. Then grieving male relatives humble themselves by dancing and singing underneath the decaying body while maggots and rotting flesh rain down upon them.

Some anthropologists argue that some missionaries misunderstood the Sawuy and Asmat, that their cultures were not based on arbitrary aggression against neighbors but on the belief that new life springs from death. They charge that Richardson and his colleagues wrote books like *Peace Child* and *Cannibal Valley* to justify foisting their fundamentalist Christian beliefs upon these people. But there is no arguing that the Sawuy, Asmat, Moni, Ekari, Dani, Damal, and the other tribal groups of Irian Jaya engaged in some unorthodox practices.

Roman Catholic missionaries, who have earned a sizable following among the Asmat, generally have taken a somewhat more sympathetic approach and provide some invaluable insights into the primitive cultures. Frank A. Trenkenschuh, an American priest with the Crosier Missions who spent years among the Asmat, wrote astutely of the clashes between the primitive and modern world that have been occurring in Irian Jaya. He said the Asmat "created a major stir when in April 1956 they killed 31 visitors from the village of Jipajer. The leaders of this killing-cannibalistic feast were sent to Merauke, for them a big city, for punishment. In fact they were given clothing, good food and a 'rich' life. When they returned to Asmat they came as influential and wealthy men who had seen the world".

It was into this volatile collision between the Stone Age and the 20th century that the restless young Rockefeller wandered with "the desire to do something adventurous" as he himself put it. Early in 1961, he spent six months with an expedition sponsored by Harvard's Peabody Museum working as a soundman on a documentary film called *Dead Birds*, a revealing look at the Dani people of the Baliem Valley. Later in the year, Rockefeller returned from a brief visit in New York to explore the Casuarina Coast and live among the Asmat.

The Asmat were already noted for their powerful, primitive fetish woodcarvings that mirrored the sanguinary ancestor and spirit-worshiping beliefs that motivated their cannibalistic cultures. For instance, the images carved on the tall, dreaded *bis* totem poles of the Asmat are those of intended victims of head-hunting sorties. Deprived of the dark, passionate motives that inspired it, much of today's Asmat art is of souvenir shop quality.

During his brief tenure in southern Irian, Rockefeller amassed an extensive selection of some of the

last examples of Asmat carving at its impressive, forceful best: three-meter long war canoes, man-sized wooden shields embellished with crocodiles and iguanas, totem poles intricately carved with ancestral figures engaged in innovative sexual activities, tall spears, drums, and, most prized and rare of all, elaborately-decorated human skulls. The collection fills an entire wing of the Museum of Primitive Art in Manhattan and there are some pieces at Jayapura's Cenderawasih University.

On November 18, 1961, Rockefeller and Dutch ethnologist René Wassing set out on an art-collecting expedition from the Catholic mission outpost of Agats in a motorized catamaran. While negotiating the treacherous currents of the Arafura Sea at the mouth of the Eilanden River, the boat was swamped and the motor drowned out. Two young Asmat guides aboard tried swimming for help. But Rockefeller and Wassing spent one night on the boat hoping to be rescued and when help did not appear the next day, they feared their guides had not reached land alive. The impatient Rockefeller decided to try it. Wassing, well aware of the strong currents, not to mention sharks and crocodiles, tried to talk him out of it. But Michael stripped to his shorts, tied his glasses around his neck, attached a red jerrican and fuel tank to his waist as floats and

dived into the sea. He was never seen again.

The Asmat guides had safely made it to shore and Wassing was soon rescued, but no trace of Michael Rockefeller has ever been found. The consensus was that the young American had drowned or been killed by sharks or crocodiles. But Michael's body was never recovered, even though his wealthy father personally supervised an exhaustive rescue operation. Tales persist that, like the guides, he too made it to shore but was killed by a fierce group of Asmat in the village of Ocenep — and was eaten. Rumors circulated that the youth's clothing, eyeglasses and skull were seen in Atsj on the Pulau River. And a Dutch priest working on the Casuarina Coast, Father Van Kessel, told an *Argosy* magazine editor that his Asmat parishioners had told him Michael Rockefeller had been killed by a chief seeking revenge for relatives killed by the Dutch.

I discussed the fascinating case with Father Bob Baudhin, an American Catholic priest who lives in Piramapun just down the coast from Agats, the very area where Rockefeller disappeared. Baudhin had lived with the Asmat for six years, spoke their complex language (there are 17 forms for the conjugation of each verb) and knew people who had been there when the mysterious events occurred. Father Bob said he had gotten the facts straight from

Dr. Kenneth Dresser, a Protestant medical doctor who had been ministering to the Asmat for decades.

"Dresser told me word was out among the Asmat that a white man had been found on the coast by a vengeful group of Asmat before anyone knew that Rockefeller was missing. None of the Asmat knew the young man had disappeared yet they were boasting to Dresser that a man matching his description had been found and killed," Father Bob said without mincing his words. "Rockefeller was definitely eaten by the Asmat in Ocenep."

About 150 kilometers up the south coast from the swamps of the Asmat is Amamapare, a modern port. It was constructed in the early 1970s to handle enormous barges from Japan and other countries. Nearby at Timika is an airport capable of accommodating contemporary jet liners. From Pad 11 at Amamapare, a heavy-duty highway slices through marshlands into the Sudirman mountains where it winds for 103 kilometers through countless switchbacks and tunnels, up glossy escarpments and sheer precipices burnished by waterfalls that evaporate into mists, to Tembagapura, a company town in crisp climes on a verdant slope at the foot of Mt. Zaagkam. It has a population of about 4,000, hospitals equipped with the latest technology, mod-

ern schools and recreational facilities. Tembagapura is Indonesian for "Coppertown."

The town, road, harbor and airport, and more than 100 million American dollars worth of infrastructure, including the world's longest single-span aerial tramway which climbs 800 meters along 1.6 kilometers of suspended cables to the mouth of a copper mine, were built by Freeport Indonesia. Freeport is a joint venture between American and Indonesian interests that are mining Gunung Bijih, "Ore Mountain," the largest above ground copper ore deposit ever discovered, an outcropping that rose 150 meters before exploitation began, extended another 340 meters below ground and contained 33 million tons of 2.5 per cent copper ore.

In 1936, a Dutch petroleum geologist, Jean Jacques Dozy, accidentally stumbled upon Gunung Bijih when he and several friends became the first to penetrate the upper reaches of the razor-backed mountain range that hugs the south coast of Irian Jaya. It was the worst possible location for a mine, 3,600 meters up a cliff. The investigation of the area by Freeport's head of exploration, Forbes Wilson, tapping of Gunung Bijih's lode by the American contractors Bechtel and Santa Fe Pomeroy were minor miracles of determination, engineering and downright dangerous work.

An aerial tramway is used to carry men up to the Freeport Indonesia copper mines high in the towering mountains that skirt the southern coastal plains of Irian Jaya (left). At a high-altitude mill, copper ore is processed into a bubbling slurry (above) so it can be pumped down a pipeline to the port.

By the time we visited Irian Jaya, Gunung Bijih had been reduced to a terraced pit 240 meters below the surface by the years of intensive mining. Boulders are pummelled into small pieces by a primary crusher at the mine site, then sent tumbling along a conveyor belt to ore-buckets on the tramway that plummets 800 meters to deposit the ore on stockpiles. A mill there processes it into a bubbling slurry that is 30 per cent copper which is pumped down a 110-kilometer pipeline to the port, converted to a dry concentrate and loaded onto barges for export. Another deposit of 46-million tons of recoverable reserves has been found only two kilometers east of Gunung Bijih that is expected to keep Freeport Indonesia contributing to the nation's economy for many more years.

Despite the proximity of modern mining technology and a city filled with enough luxuries to keep more than 100 Americans and their families happy, the area's original inhabitants, mainly Damal and Moni, continue to live much as they have for centuries. Because of the poor soils, they practice swidden agriculture, growing tubers like yams and sweet potatoes, the staples of Irian Jaya's highland peoples, and some vegetables and fruits. They also hunt small game and are expert marksmen with homemade wooden arrows and bows.

Naturally, there have been adjustment problems between the mining operation and the local people who have suddenly found themselves propelled from the Stone Age into the 20th century, bypassing the intermediate eras that the rest of mankind has evolved through. But there have been positive effects as well. Freeport buys some 20 tons of vegetables from the people of the mountain villages and ten tons of fish from coastal peoples every month. Company helicopters, which usually have to complete their runs before noon each morning when swirling mists pussyfoot into the mountains and make flying hazardous (our American-born helicopter pilot Wayne Knight pointed out the wreckage of two planes that had nosed into Puncak Jaya just below its glistening glacier during World War II) are no longer mysterious harbingers to be feared, but bringers of cash and, more importantly, medicine, additional food, tools and other needs that have improved the quality of their lives.

The largest indigenous group in Irian Jaya, and the most studied, proselytized to and fawned over by tourists are the Dani. About 100,000 Dani live in the Baliem Valley, once known simultaneously as "Cannibal Valley" and "Shangri-la," and another 100,000 are spread through the rugged highlands

The men of most of Irian Jaya's numerous ethnic groups have traditionally been warriors with a fierce streak, reflected in the expression of the man (above), whose cultures revolved around tribal wars, head-hunting and cannibalism. Indonesian authorities have attempted to channel destructive energies into competitive sports like a game of soccer at Tembagapura (top left).

A Dani man of Irian Jaya wears a headdress of cassowary bird feathers and animal teeth.
Numbering about 200,000, the Dani are the largest indigenous group in the province.
About half of them inhabit the magnificent Grand Valley of the Baliem River and the rest
live in the rugged mountains to the west, far from the modern world.

west of the valley. Considering all the attention they have received from Protestant missionaries, anthropologists, government officials and, most recently, tourists, since their valley was "discovered" in 1938, the Dani have remained stubbornly loyal to many of their traditions and habits.

One of the most obvious is the men's predilection for wearing nothing but a long, narrow vegetable gourd known as a *koteka*, as Indonesians call it, or *holim* in the Dani language, which is slipped over the penis but leaves everything else exposed. The government mounted a campaign called *Operation Koteka* in the mid-seventies to encourage the men to trade in their gourds for short pants, but it did not prove overly successful and the *koteka* remains popular attire even in Wamena, the government's nerve center in the Baliem Valley. Danis clad in *koteka* adorned with feathers or flower petals stroll through the streets alongside government employees in office attire. Many Dani women still wear only strings of beads on their hips and grass skirts. Men and women also wear mesh hairnets that are used to carry loads of sweet potatoes, personal belongings, even piglets and infants. The lack of attire among the Danis is all the more startling considering their homelands are 1,700 meters or more above sea level and temperatures usually drop to 10 degrees centigrade or cooler in the evenings or during the frequent afternoon rains. The Danis smear themselves with pig's grease and sleep cuddled up to each other around fires in communal huts, the men with the men, women with other women and children.

From one of the Twin Otters or Casa Aviocars that Merpati Nusantara Airlines flies into Wamena, the Grand Baliem Valley is the phenomenal site that inspired comparisons with Shangri-la. The planes fly through tight mountain passes and the clouds open suddenly onto a beautiful green valley 70 kilometers long and 15-kilometers wide split by the silvery Baliem River, peppered with the domed thatch huts of the Danis and checkered with irrigated patches of sweet potatoes and vegetables fenced off from each other.

Except for a few new roads, the view is almost the same one that thrilled American adventurer Richard Archibold when he spotted the valley and landed on the Baliem in a seaplane in June, 1938. Droves of missionaries, mostly Protestants, followed on foot and in planes. The accounts of their exploits make fascinating reading. In *Cannibal Valley*, Russell T. Hitt quoted from a letter written from one missionary family to friends back home in Florida: "In the States when we wanted to relax, we drove downtown to the Dairy Queen for some ice cream. Now, we go down to Elisa and Ruth's and watch a pig killing." While their motivations and some of their methods may be debatable, the missionaries must be given credit, not just for their courage and fortitude, but for deciphering complex languages and providing insights into the cultures of Irian Jaya.

The Danis, like the Asmat, traditionally worshiped their ancestors and engaged in endless rounds of warfare to avenge the deaths of comrades killed in battle. They worked themselves into screaming, violent frenzies in spear-rattling dances wearing cassowary feathers, bones in their noses and warpaint, before confronting the enemy. According to some accounts, victims were dismembered and cannibalized, the ultimate humiliation in Dani society. Women and children mourning the deaths of relatives customarily amputated their fingers to the first joint and smeared themselves with mud.

The greatest warriors rose to become village leaders and boasted many barkcloth strips of cowrie shells, the local currency, and dozens of wives and pigs. Pigs are so prized they are treated like members of the families and live under the women's quarters. Wars between neighboring villages sometimes lasted for decades until the same number of men had died on each side. Missionaries sometimes got caught in the skirmishes or became the objects of attack. Two Americans, Stan Dale and Phil Masters, were killed by Yali tribesmen in 1968. Missionaries have attempted to pacify the people with Christianity, while the Indonesian government has tried to channel the warrior spirit into competitive contact sports like soccer and boxing. The results have been mixed. In fact, while we were in Irian Jaya, 14 Danis died during a battle with axes and arrows over land rights in a village near Wamena.

Back in Jayapura, I discussed the issue of cultural change with Dr. August Kafiar, an associate rector of the University of Cenderawasih, who was born in Irian Jaya on Biak island and studied in the United States. "Our world becomes smaller and smaller so it is difficult for any one group or tribe to avoid adapting to and also adopting modern cultures. The important thing I think is to be able to adjust in such a way that the changes and new cultures will have a positive influence," Dr. Kafiar said.

"When you talk about 'culture shock' here in Irian, it has been brought on not only by foreigners but by people from other areas of Indonesia so the people here get frustrated because they face a double problem," he added. "We are working hard to bridge the gaps between our cultures. Every culture has its good and bad points. It's a matter of us holding onto the good things in our cultures and selecting the good things from the new ones."

The early evening of the second and fourth Friday of every month is an exciting time in Jayapura. That is when the *Km. Umsini*, one of the *Rinjani's* sister ships, cruises into town for the last stop on a seven day voyage all the way from Jakarta with stops in Sorong, Ternate, Bitung in North Sulawesi, Ujung Pandang, and Surabaya. When the *Umsini* blasts its horn and glides into the harbor, the people of Jayapura drop what they are doing and come out from their homes on the hills of the town to watch. On the horizon, the Pacific swallows the sun and the *Umsini* turns into a carousel of twinkling lights. The people trickle downtown, whole familes of them, to the wharf where the ship docks to clamber around its decks and wait in the boarding hall among mountains of baggage and throngs of relatives.

Kal and I, clutching bows and arrows and other souvenirs, shoved our way good-naturedly into the hall and fortified ourselves in a niche in the small canteen to await the boarding call, lubricating the passing of the hours with Bintang beer. Along the way, we were slapped on our sweaty backs by grinning people, begged to join a group of happy hard drinkers and gawked at. It was the usual chaos we had been through so many times before.

It did not matter. We were in high spirits, homeward bound after five months of travel. The passage back to Jakarta aboard the *Umsini* was a fitting way to go, slowly, stopping at ports we had come to know intimately during the years, savoring each day and night on the archipelago's sultry seas, content in the knowledge that there would always be another paradise island in Indonesia waiting for us around the next bend of the equator.

The beauty — and mystery — that makes all of Indonesia's
islands so alluring is reflected in the dramatic contrasts of Irian
Jaya's landscapes. There are forbidding swamps in the south (top)
and inviting beaches like Base G on the north coast (bottom). And
even though it rises in the tropics, Puncak Jaya (following pages)
is so tall it has a permanent snowcap.

THAILAND

BANGKOK

SOUTH CHINA SEA

MANILA

Gulf of Thailand

Sulu Sea

SABANG

Penang

BANDA ACEH

Lhokseumawe

KOTA KINABALU

Bandar Seri Begawan

SABAH

MALAYSIA (WEST)

BRUNEI

MEDAN

Lake Toba

KUALA LUMPUR

MALAYSIA (EAST)

Tarakan

Straits of Malacca

Natuna Islands

Sibolga

MALACCA

SARAWAK

NIAS

SINGAPORE

KUCHING

SUMATRA

Riau Archipelago

PONTIANAK

Mahakam River

Bukittinggi

PADANG

Kapuas River

BORNEO (KALIMANTAN)

Tenggarong

Samarinda

PALU

Mentawai Islands

JAMBI

BALIKPAPAN

BANGKA

Palangka Raya

Barito River

SULAWE

PALEMBANG

Rantepao

Bengkulu

Cape Puting
Nature Reserve

BANJARMASIN

Straits of Macassar

Lake P

Java Sea

TELUKBETUNG

UJUNG PANDANG

Watam

Krakatau

Sunda Straits

JAKARTA

Flores Sea

Tamba

Bogor

SEMARANG

MADURA

Ujung Kulon
National Park

Kaduketug

BANDUNG

SURABAYA

Komodo

YOGYAKARTA

Mt. Bromo

BALI

Lombok

Fl

INDIAN OCEAN

JAVA

DENPASAR

Sumbawa

Sumba

LESSER SUNDA

Indonesia

*A Map of the Archipelago and surrounding Countries
incorporating some of the Places visited by the Author
and Photographer during the Course of their Travels.*

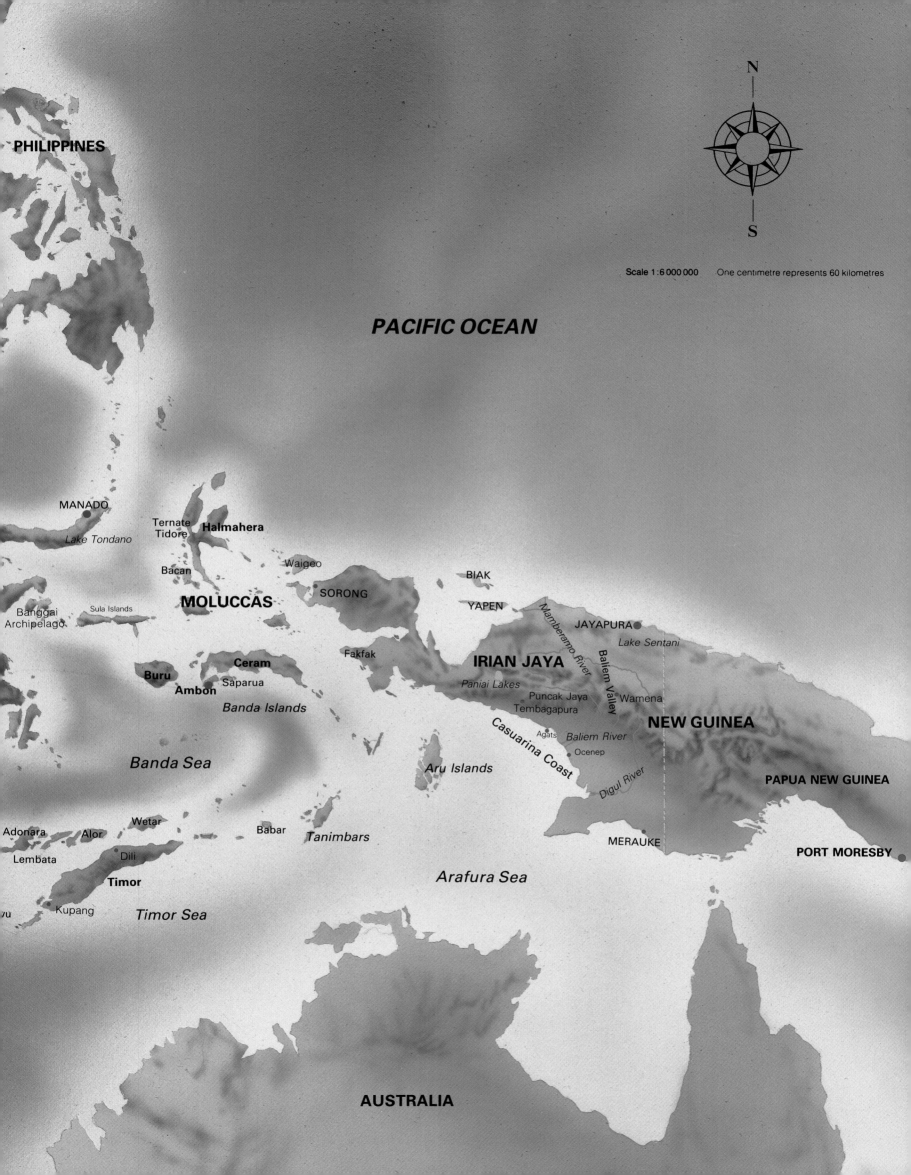

Bibliography

Abdurachman, Paramita R. "New Winds, New Forces." *Prisma, The Indonesian Indicator.* Institute for Economic and Social Research, Education and Information: Jakarta, No. 33, September, 1984.

Alisjahbana, Takdir S. *Indonesia: Social and Cultural Revolution.* Oxford University Press: Oxford, 1966.

American Women's Association. *Introducing Indonesia.* Jakarta, Fourth Edition, Second Printing, 1984.

A Thousand Faces of Jakarta: CV Noni Depok: Jakarta, 1984.

Atlas van Tropisch Nederland. 's-Gravenhage. Various Issues.

van Baal, J.; Galis, K.W. and Koentjaraningat, R.M. *West Irian: A Bibliography.* Koninklijk Institut Voortall-, Land-, en Volkenkunde; Foris Publications: Dordrecht, Biblio. Series 15, 1984.

Baum, Vicki. *A Tale from Bali.* Geoffrey Bles: London, 1937. Oxford University Press: Oxford, 1973.

Bock, Carl. *The Head-Hunters of Borneo: A Narrative of Travel up the Mahakkam and down the Barito; also, Journeyings in Sumatra.* 2nd ed. Sampson, Low, Marston, Searle & Rivington, 1882.

Boyce, David. *Kutai, East Kalimantan: A Journal of Past and Present Glory.* Kota Bangun, 1983.

Boxer, C.R. *Jan Compagnie in War and Peace 1602–1799: A Short History of the Dutch East-India Company.* Heinemann Asia: Hong Kong, 1979.

van den Broek, J.A. *De Portugueezen in de Molukken (1511–1677).* The Hague, 1897.

Brooke, James. *Narrative of Events in Borneo and Celebes down to the Occupation of Labuan: From the Journals of James Brooke, Esq.* 2 vols. John Murray: London, 1848.

Bunge, Frederica M. *Indonesia: A Country Study.* The American University: Washington, D.C. 1983.

Conrad, Joseph. *Almayer's Folly: A Story of an Eastern River and Tales of Unrest.*

———. *Lord Jim.* Doubleday & Company, Inc.: New York, 1900. Bantam Books: Toronto, 1981.

Crawfurd, John. *A Descriptive Dictionary of the Indian Islands and Adjacent Countries.* London, 1856.

Covarrubias, Miguel. *Island of Bali.* Alfred A. Knopf: New York, 1937. Oxford University Press: Oxford, 1972.

Dalton, Bill. *Indonesia Handbook.* Moon Publications: Chico, California, Third Edition, 1985.

de Wit, Augusta. *Java: Facts and Fancies.* W.P. van Stockum: The Hague, 1912. Oxford University Press: Oxford, 1984.

Dick, Gerry. "Where the Ice Age Lingers." *Panorama.* Brisbane, December, 1984, No. 31.

"Galunggung Volcano: Its Horrifying Eruption and Effect on the Surrounding Areas." *Indonesia Magazine.* Yayasan Harapan Kita: Jakarta, No. 7, 1983.

Geertz, Clifford. *The Religion of Java.* Glencoe Free Press: Illinois, 1960.

———. *Peddlers and Princes: Social Change and Economic Modernization in Two Indonesian Towns.* University of Chicago Press: Chicago, 1963.

Gibbons, Alice. *The People Time Forgot.* Moody Press: Chicago, 1981.

Hadmoko, Daisy, ed. *Travel Indonesia.* P.T. Travia Duta: Jakarta. Various issues, July 1979–March, 1986.

Hall, D.G.E. *A History of Southeast Asia.* St. Martin's Press: New York, Third Edition, 1976.

Hamzah, Rochmuljati (trans.). *Bung Hata's Answers (Menjawab Jakarta, 1978).* Gunung Agung: Jakarta, 1981.

Hanbury Tenison, Maria. *A Slice of Spice: Travels to the Indonesian Islands.* Hutchinson of London: 1974.

Hanbury Tenison, Robin. *A Pattern of Peoples: A Journey among the Tribes of the Outer Indonesian Islands.* Angus and Robinson: London, 1975.

Hanna, Willard A. *Bali Chronicle.*

———. *Indonesian Banda.* Institute for the Study of Human Issues, Inc.: Philadelphia, 1978.

———. *Jakarta Chronicle: From Pepper Port to Megalopolis.*

Hardjono, J. *Indonesia, Land and People.* Gunung Agung: Jakarta, 1971.

Hitt, Russell T. *Cannibal Valley.* Hodder & Stoughton: London, 1962.

Heuken, A. *Historical Sites of Jakarta.* Cipta Loka Caraka: Jakarta, 1982.

Huehn, Kurt Goetz. *Indonesia, Hildebrand's Travel Guide: Vol. 6.* K+G. KARTO+GRAFIK Verlagsges. mbH: Frankfurt, 1985.

"Irian Jaya". *Pacific Islands Yearbook 1985.*

Ismartono, Yuli. "Island-Hopping in North Maluku." *Travel Indonesia.* P.T. Travia Duta: Jakarta. Vol 2, No. 10, October, 1980.

Jones, Howard Palfrey. *Indonesia: The Possible Dream.* Ayu Mas: Singapore, 1971.

Kayam, Umar. "My Wife, Madame Schlitz and the Monster," *Sri Sumarah and Other Stories.* Translated by Harry Aveling. Heinemann Asia: Kuala Lumpur, 1980.

de Klerk, Edward Servaas. *History of the Netherlands East Indies.* 2 Vols. Rotterdam: 1938.

Koch, C.J. *The Year of Living Dangerously.* Sphere Books Ltd.: 1981.

Koentjaraningrat (ed.) *Villages in Indonesia.* Cornell University Press: New York, 1967.

Komroff, Manuel, ed. *The Travels of Marco Polo.* Revised and edited from Marsden's Translation. Liveright Inc.: New York, 1982.

"Kumpulan Lagu-lagu Rakyat Irian Jaya." Lembaga Antropologi Universitas Cenderawasih: Jayapura, 1980.

Kunst, Jaap. *Hindu-Javanese Musical Instruments.* Martinus Nijhoff: The Hague, 1968.

Lee Khoon Choy. *Indonesia: Between Myth and Reality.* Federal Publications: Singapore, 1977.

Legge, J.D. *Sukarno: A Political Biography.* Penguin Books: Harmondsworth, Middlesex, 1973.

———. *Indonesia.* Prentice Hall of Australia: Sydney, Second Edition, 1977.

Llewellyn, Philip. "Camel Trophy '85: Braving the Jungles of Kalimantan." *Garuda Magazine.* Vol. 5, No. 4, 1985.

Loeb, Edwin M. *Sumatra: Its History and People.* Verlag des Institutes fur Volkerkunde der Universitat, Wien: 1935. Oxford University Press: Oxford, 1972.

Lubis, Mochtar. *Twilight in Jakarta.* Hutchinson: London, 1963. Oxford University Press: Oxford.

———. *The Indonesian Dilemma.* Trans. by F. Lamoureux. Graham Brash: Singapore, 1983.

Machlin, Milt. *The Search for Michael Rockefeller.* G.P., Putnam and Sons: New York, 1972.

Marampa, A.T. *A Guide to Toraja.* Rantepao, 1974.

Marsden, William. *The History of Sumatra Containing an Account of the Government, Laws, Customs, and Manners of the Native Inhabitants with a Description of the Natural Productions, and a Relation of the Ancient Political State of that Island.* 3rd ed. J.M. Creery, Black-Horse-Court: London, 1811. Oxford University Press: Oxford, 1971.

Masselman, George. *The Cradle of Colonialism.* Yale University Press: New Haven, 1963.

———. *The Money Trees: The Spice Trade.* New York, 1967.

Maxwell, Robyn. "Textiles and Tusks: Some Observations on the Social Dimensions of Weaving in East Flores." *Five Essays on the Indonesian Arts: Music, Theater, Textiles, Painting and Literature.* Monash University: Australia, 1981.

McVey, Ruth T. (ed.) *Indonesia.* HRAF Press: New Haven, 1963.

"Minangkabau." *Indonesia Magazine*. Indoma Jaya Pte. Ltd.: Jakarta.

McPhee, Colin. *A House in Bali*. Victor Gollancz Ltd.: London, 1947. Oxford University Press: Oxford, 1979.

Mears, Leon A. "Rice and Food Self-Sufficiency in Indonesia." *Bulletin of Indonesian Economic Studies*. Australian National University: Canberra, Vol. 20, No. 2. August 1984.

Mikloucho-Maclay, Nikolai Nikolaevich. *New Guinea Diaries, 1871–1883*. Kristen Pres, Inc: Jakarta. 1975.

Moor, J.H., ed. *Notices of the Indian Archipelago and Adjacent Countries: Being a Collection of Papers Relating to Borneo, Celebes, Bali, Java, Sumatra, Nias, the Philippine Islands, Sulus, Siam, Cochin China, Malayan Peninsula, etc.* Singapore, 1837.

Mulder, Niels. *Mysticism and Everyday Life in Contemporary Java: Cultural Persistence and Change*. Singapore University Press: Singapore, 1978.

Multatuli. *Max Havelaar or The Coffee Sales of the Netherlands Trading Company*. Trans. by W. Siebenhaar. Alfred A. Knopf: New York, 1927. Macmillan and Southdene: Selangor and Kuala Lumpur, 1984.

Neill, Wilfred T. *Twentieth-Century Indonesia*. Columbia University Press: New York, 1973.

Noer, Deliar. *The Modern Muslim Movement in Indonesia, 1900–1942*. Oxford University Press: Oxford, 1973.

Oey, Eric, ed. *Indonesia*. Apa Productions Insight Guides: Singapore, 1985.

O'Hanlon, Redmond. *Into the Heart of Borneo*. Penguin Books: Middlesex, 1985.

Penders, C.L.M. *The Life and Times of Sukarno*. Oxford University Press: Kuala Lumpur, 1975.

Pireś, Tome. "The Suma Oriental of Tome Pireś: An Account of the East, from the Red Sea to Japan, Written in Malacca and India in 1511–1515 and the Book of Francisco Rodrigues (Trans and Edited by Armando Cortesao)." *The Hakluyt Society, London*. Second Series, No. 89, Vol. 1 & 2. 1944.

Plage, Dieter and Mary. "In the Shadow of Krakatau: The Return of Java's Wildlife." National Geographic: Washington, June, 1985.

Powell, Hickman. *The Last Paradise*. Jonathan Cape and Harrison Smith Inc.: New York, 1930. Oxford University Press: Oxford, 1982.

Radjab, Muhamad. *Dongengang Sulawesi Selatan*. Jakarta, 1950.

Raffles, Thomas Stamford: *The History of Java*. 3 Vols, Black, Parbury, London, 1817. 2 Vols, Oxford University Press: Oxford, 1965.

Reid, Anthony. *The Contest for North Sumatra: Aceh, the Netherlands and Britain 1858–1898*. Oxford University Press: Kuala Lumpur, Singapore, 1969.

Richardson, Don. *Peace Child*. G/L Regal Books: Glendale, CA, 1974.

Ricklefs, M.C. *A History of Modern Indonesia*. The Macmillan Press Ltd.: London, 1981.

Rockefeller, Michael. *The Asmat*. Museum of Primitive Art: New York, 1964.

Roeder, O.G. *The Smiling General: President Suharto of Indonesia*. Gunung Agung: Jakarta, 1969.

Sandarupa, Drs. Stanislaus. *Life and Death of the Toraja People*. Ujung Pandang, 1984.

Saulnier, Tony. *Headhunters of Papua*. Crown Publishers Inc.: New York, 1962.

Silalahi, Richard A. "Eradicating Poverty through Transmigration. *Jakarta Post*. August 12, 1985.

Silzer, Peter James. "Irian Jaya: Linguistic Research 1975–1985 with proposals for the future." Lembaga Ekonomi dan Kemasyarakatan Nasional.

Slametmuljana. *A Story of Majapahit*. Singapore University Press: Singapore, 1976.

Smithies, Michael. *A Javanese Boyhood: An Ethnographic Biography*. Federal Publications: Singapore, 1982.

Specter, Michael. "A Sprawling, Thirsty Giant." *Far Eastern Economic Review*. Hong Kong, March 29, 1984.

Steinbauer, Friedrich. *Melanesian Cargo Cults*. University of Queensland Press: 1979.

Stuart Fox, David J. *Once a Century: Pura Besakih and the Eka Dasa Rudra Festival*. Penerbit Sinar Harapan and Citra Indonesia: Jakarta, 1982.

Sukarno. *Sukarno: An Autobiography*. As told to Cindy Adams. Gunung Agung: Jakarta, 1966.

Sumaamidjaja, Koswara. "Indonesian Painting: In Search of Recognition." *Five Essays on the Indonesian Arts: Music, Theater, Textiles, Painting and Literature*. Monash University: Australia, 1981.

Székely, Ladislao. *Tropic Fever: The Adventures of a Planter in Sumatra*. Harper & Brothers: 1937. Oxford University Press: Oxford, 1978.

Tangdilintin, L.T. and Syafei, M. *Toraja: An Introduction to Unique Culture*. Yayasan Lepongan Bulan: Rantepao, 1983.

Tarrant, Bill. "The Great Bug Safari." *Asia Magazine*: Hong Kong, January 26, 1986.

Trenkenschuh, Frank A., editor. *Asmat Sketchbook*. Crosier Missions: Hastings, NE, Vols 1–8.

Veen, H. van der. "Sa'dan-Toradja'sche Volksverhalen." *Verhandelingen Bataviaasch Genootschap van Kunsten en Wetenschappen:* Vol. 65, Part 2, 1924.

————. "The Sa'dan Toradja Chant for the Deceased." *Verhandelingen van het Koninklijk Insituut voor Taal-, Land- en Volkenkunde:* 1966, Vol. 49.

Wall, Kaarin. *A Jakarta Market*. American's Women Association: Jakarta, 1983.

Wallace, Alfred Russel. *The Malay Archipelago: The Land of the Orang-utan and the Bird of Paradise: A Narrative of Travel with Studies of Man and Nature*. Macmillan and Company, London, 1869. Reprinted Dover Publications, Inc.: New York, 1962.

Wertheim, W.F. *Indonesian Society in Transition*. Van Hoeve: The Hague, 1956.

Wilhelm, Donald. *Emerging Indonesia*. Indira: Jakarta, 1980.

Williams, Maslyn. *Five Journeys from Jakarta: Inside Sukarno's Indonesia*. Morrow: New York, 1965.

Woldendorp, Richard; Johns, A.H. and Johns, Y. *Indonesia*. Thomas Nelson Australia Ltd: Sydney, 1972.

Wolters, O.W. *Early Indonesian Commerce: A Study of the Origins of Srivijaya*. Cornell University Press: Ithaca, 1967.

Young, Ken. "Minangkabau Authority Patterns and the Effects of Dutch Rule." *The Malay-Islamic World of Sumatra: Studies in Politics and Culture*. Monash University: 1982.

Zach, Paul. "Floridian in Paradise." *The Floridian*. Times Publishing Co.: St. Petersburg, Sept. 27, 1981.

————. "Indonesia." *International Herald Tribune*, June 6, 1986.

————. "Indonesia Begins Relocating People." *The Washington Post*. July 11, 1979.

————. "Jakarta, Jakarta." *Winds*. Japan Air Lines: Tokyo. September, 1985.

————. "Letter from Bali: In A Tourist Spectacular, Bali Town Burns a King." *The Washington Post*. February 7, 1979.

————. "Letter from Bali: Sacrifices at a Volcano in a Colorful Quest for Peace." *The Washington Post*. May 1, 1979.

————. "Our Man in Indonesia." *Writer's Yearbook*. Writer's Digest Publications: Cincinnati, Vol. 53, 1982.

Zoete, Beryl de and Spies, Walter. *Dance and Drama in Bali*. Faber and Faber: London, 1938. Oxford University Press: Oxford, 1973.

Index/Glossary

237

Photographer Kal Muller uses his underwater Nikonos to photograph a sacred eel in the spring of Waai on the island of Ambon (top). Author Paul Zach interviews M.J. Somphie on the roof of the bridge of Indonesia's enormous passenger vessel, the *Km. Rinjani*, as it glides through the Salawati Straits of Irian Jaya (bottom).

Acknowledgements

During our travels in Indonesia we looked up dozens of old friends and made hundreds of new ones, many of whom contributed their knowledge and expertise to this book. It is impossible to mention everyone, but we would especially like to thank the following:

Joop Ave, Director General of Tourism and Dra. Cri Murthi, Director of Marketing of Tourism; and Udin Saifuddin, Hs. Dalimunthe, Sembiring and the rest of the staff of the Department of Tourism in Jakarta and in the provinces; Dr. Mochtar Kusumaatmadja, Minister of Foreign Affairs.

Also to Drs. Daniel S. Sahusilawane and Laribu Meoko and the Department of Information; Des Alwi; Bouraq Indonesian Airways; Michael Scheutzendorf, Beranti Ismail and the entire management and staff of the Jakarta Hilton International; Herman Diener and the Hotel Benakutai in Balikpapan; Pak Muis of the district cultural office and Pak Budiarjo of the tourism office of Samarinda; Haris Surono of the Kutai National Park; the Makassar Golden Hotel; Petta Ballasari and the Hotel A. Pada in Sengkang/Wajo; Nico B. Pasaka and Indonesia Safari Travel in Ujung Pandang; Loky Herlambang and the Nusantara Diving Center, the management of the Kawanua City Hotel and government tourist board in Menado; Dr Axel Ridder of Hotel Krakatau; Admiral Urip Santoso of P.T. Tourdevco; Sasmiyarsi Sasmoyo of Bali Indonesia Murni Ltd.; Jack Daniels of P.T. Lumba Lumba Permai; Sjafwan Kausal (Iwan) at Parpostel, Ibu Sitanala and the Hotel Mutiara, Ambon; and Jusuf Chon in Jayapura and Imrad Idris, Iain MacGregor and Wayne Knight of Freeport Indonesia in Tembagapura, Irian Jaya; and to Garuda Indonesia airlines.

Finally our thanks to Woon Mee Lan at Times Editions who spent so many hours putting this book together.

Terima kasih banyak,
Paul and Kal